Stephen Colbert

Stephen Colbert

by Bonnie Szumski and Jill Karson

LUCENT BOOKS
A part of Gale, Cengage Learning

GALE
CENGAGE Learning·

Detroit • New York • San Francisco • New Haven, Conn • Waterville, Maine • London

LIBRARY OF CONGRESS CATALOGING-IN-PUBLICATION DATA

Szumski, Bonnie, 1958-
  Stephen Colbert / by Bonnie Szumski and Jill Karson.
    p. cm. -- (People in the news)
  Includes bibliographical references and index.
  ISBN 978-1-4205-0617-4 (hardcover)
  1. Colbert, Stephen--Juvenile literature. 2. Comedians--United States--Biography--Juvenile literature. 3. Actors--United States--Biography--Juvenile literature. 4. Television personalities--United States--Biography--Juvenile literature. I. Karson, Jill. II. Title.
  PN2287.C5695S97 2012
  792.702'8092--dc23
  [B]
                                                                    2011041999

Lucent Books
27500 Drake Rd
Farmington Hills MI 48331

ISBN-13: 978-1-4205-0617-4
ISBN-10: 1-4205-0617-X

Printed in the United States of America
1 2 3 4 5 6 7 16 15 14 13 12

Contents

Fame and celebrity are alluring. People are drawn to those who walk in fame's spotlight, whether they are known for great accomplishments or for notorious deeds. The lives of the famous pique public interest and attract attention, perhaps because their experiences seem in some ways so different from, yet in other ways so similar to, our own.

Newspapers, magazines, and television regularly capitalize on this fascination with celebrity by running profiles of famous people. For example, television programs such as *Entertainment Tonight* devote all their programming to stories about entertainment and entertainers. Magazines such as *People* fill their pages with stories of the private lives of famous people. Even newspapers, newsmagazines, and television news frequently delve into the lives of well-known personalities. Despite the number of articles and programs, few provide more than a superficial glimpse at their subjects.

Lucent's People in the News series offers young readers a deeper look into the lives of today's newsmakers, the influences that have shaped them, and the impact they have had in their fields of endeavor and on other people's lives. The subjects of the series hail from many disciplines and walks of life. They include authors, musicians, athletes, political leaders, entertainers, entrepreneurs, and others who have made a mark on modern life and who, in many cases, will continue to do so for years to come.

These biographies are more than factual chronicles. Each book emphasizes the contributions, accomplishments, or deeds that have brought fame or notoriety to the individual and shows how that person has influenced modern life. Authors portray their subjects in a realistic, unsentimental light. For example, Bill Gates—the cofounder and former chief executive officer of the software giant Microsoft—has been instrumental in making personal computers the most vital tool of the modern age. Few dispute his business savvy, his perseverance, or his technical expertise, yet critics say he is ruthless in his dealings with competitors and driven more by his desire to maintain Microsoft's dominance in the computer industry than by an interest in furthering technology.

In these books, young readers will encounter inspiring stories about real people who achieved success despite enormous obstacles. Oprah Winfrey—one of the most powerful, most watched, and wealthiest women in television history—spent the first six years of her life in the care of her grandparents while her unwed mother sought work and a better life elsewhere. Her adolescence was colored by pregnancy at age fourteen, rape, and sexual abuse.

Each author documents and supports his or her work with an array of primary and secondary source quotations taken from diaries, letters, speeches, and interviews. All quotes are footnoted to show readers exactly how and where biographers derive their information and provide guidance for further research. The quotations enliven the text by giving readers eyewitness views of the life and accomplishments of each person covered in the People in the News series.

In addition, each book in the series includes photographs, annotated bibliographies, timelines, and comprehensive indexes. For both the casual reader and the student researcher, the People in the News series offers insight into the lives of today's newsmakers—people who shape the way we live, work, and play in the modern age.

A New Twist on an Old Concept

Fools or court jesters were clownish figures kept by kings and queens in English courts during the Renaissance. Part entertainer, part counselor, and part satirical truth teller, a fool could and did become an important member of a monarch's entourage. Because the fool was given leniency by a king or queen, he could deliver bad news about how the people were feeling toward the monarch without fear of punishment. The fool also used a mixture of humor and satire to gently poke fun at the monarch, though good-natured barbs were pointed enough that the monarch always got the joke. The monarch often relied on such shrewd commentary as needed perspective on his or her rule. In fact, Queen Elizabeth is said to have been upset with her fool for being too soft on her.

In much the same way, Stephen Colbert plays the nation's fool. He himself has used the analogy, calling the character he plays "a fool who has spent a lot of his life playing not the fool."[1] By good-naturedly mocking (and exposing the hypocrisy of) the mainstream media, politicians, and others, he makes pointed commentary on how those in power attempt to both manipulate and win the trust of the American public.

Scathing, Smart Commentary

Colbert pokes fun at these figures and a vast array of topics— including religion, politics, sexuality, culture, racism, homophobia, marketing, hypocrisy, health, the media, technology, and

Colbert's absurd political commentator persona has made him a comedy star.

more—in biting satire. Four nights a week on Comedy Central's *The Colbert Report*, very few escape his scathing, smart commentary, all delivered under the auspices of his harmless news anchor personality. When he delivers monologues, he uses offensive, absurd statements to point out the absurdity and offensiveness of people who hold such views. He uses deadpan, error-filled observations to make light of the more ridiculous and unbelievable aspects of contemporary society. When he conducts interviews,

Colbert can be pure clown, asking absurd questions of his guest. At the same time, he often asks pointed, clever questions that clearly reveal both his level of knowledge on a topic and the lack of critical thinking on the part of his interviewee. This combination of zaniness and cunning proves a winning combination that entertains as much as it illuminates.

The popularity of his show and his character has proven that Americans love and need their fool. His accolades have been serious and prestigious: Colbert was named one of *Time* magazine's 100 Most Influential People in 2006. He has also received Emmy awards, Peabody awards, and an honorary doctorate degree from Knox College. He has also reaped numerous silly honors and fun awards in the pop culture realm: for example, he has his own Ben & Jerry's ice cream flavor (Americone Dream) and a namesake aircraft in the Virgin America fleet (Air Colbert). Whether the awards he has received are serious or silly, all serve to show the many ways in which the American public has embraced him, and on a variety of levels.

Many of these honors are the work of his active fan base, whom Colbert has dubbed the Colbert Nation. They regularly rally around his causes and eagerly follow whatever mission he gives them, whether it be editing websites to reflect Colbert's opinion, or submitting his name to have ships, buildings, or mascots named after him. Colbert's fans are so responsive to his orders, in fact, that the media has dubbed the way they respond to the products and people he promotes as the "Colbert bump." The idea refers to the increase in sales, popularity, or notoriety people or products receive if Colbert promotes them. In this way, Colbert definitely wields more than a comedian's influence, and he enjoys the role so much that he will actually refer to the phenomenon on the show should a guest underestimate the power of his fans' loyalty.

The Truth About Stephen Colbert

Colbert's status as a pop culture icon and his professional persona as a silly prankster or pompous idiot masks his sharp wit and intellectual approach to comedy. He makes astute observations about American society; he mocks politicians, the political system, corporate America, and the media with such biting clarity that it is sometimes hard to tell the joke from reality. Above all, Colbert enjoys playing with words and language. Many of his jokes examine how phrases and concepts are used, what they mean to contemporary culture. They also highlight the concepts Americans take for granted when they use language without thinking about it.

At the heart of many of his jokes are smart and fascinating observations about the American condition and deep, philosophical concepts of truth, reason, liberty, and freedom. "Colbert regularly plays around with concepts that are near and dear to the philosopher's heart, concepts such as Truth and Reality," writes Aaron Allen Schiller in *Stephen Colbert and Philosophy: I Am Philosophy (And So Can You!)*. "In fact, let me hazard a prediction here and say that from this day forth no philosophical tract on the nature of Truth will be complete without some consideration to the concept of truthiness."[2] Colbert's ability to call attention to America's philosophical and political struggles in a smart, satirical, and hilarious way remains his most profound legacy.

Chapter 1

The Tragic Road to Comedy

Stephen Colbert credits much of his comic tendencies to early childhood tragedy. He believes his desire to make people laugh stems from the heartbreaking death of his father and two siblings in a plane crash when Colbert was just ten years old. The tragedy left him with a deep desire to cheer up his mother. The role of alleviating the sadness of the household stuck with him and would eventually become a career. Although his early years were marked by tragedy, they were also shaped by a solid, close family deeply rooted in religion and humor.

A Large Family

Stephen Tyrone Colbert was born on May 13, 1964, in Washington, D.C., but grew up just outside of Charleston, South Carolina, on rural James Island. The family's home was located off a dirt road. As a small boy, he took full advantage of the rural lifestyle, and enjoyed riding bikes, fishing, and playing with friends. He had an Irish-Catholic upbringing in a large family of eleven children. He was the youngest of eight sons and three daughters.

His father, James William Colbert Jr., was a doctor of immunology as well as the overseer of academic affairs at the Medical University of South Carolina. Colbert's colleagues at MUSC speak highly of him, recalling a gentle man. They also mention his sense of humor, which may have influenced his son: "The ... time

Colbert attends the Sundance Film Festival in January 2005. His upbringing was out of the Hollywood limelight, as he grew up in rural James Island, South Carolina, the youngest of eleven children in his family.

shared at MUSC was memorable for his gifted leadership and unflagging commitment to building a fine academic institution, a goal kept on course by his decisiveness, limitless energy, high integrity and a ready good humor."[3]

Stephen's mother, Lorna, was an aspiring actress who set aside her professional ambitions to raise her children as a homemaker. Colbert has described her as being larger than life. His later thespian leanings probably started with her. Having a witty father and an actress for a mother meant that Stephen was exposed early on to word play and role playing.

Religious Upbringing

Although Stephen's parents were devout Catholics, his parents allowed for questioning on issues of faith. Colbert says: "I love my Church, and I'm a Catholic who was raised by

Pronunciation of Colbert

Today, Stephen Colbert pronounces his name col-BEAR, although originally, the name was pronounced COL-bert, with a hard t at the end. He debated changing the pronunciation of his name for many years, but it was not until he was on a flight to Chicago to attend Northwestern University's prestigious theater program that he decided to embrace the alternate pronunciation for good. He recalls that his father had given him and his siblings a choice in the matter: "My dad always wanted to be Col-BEAR ... so [he] said to us, 'You can be anything you want.' And so we made a choice, and it's about half and half. The girls for the most part are like, 'Get over it, you're Colbert,' but I was so young when this choice was given to us, I think that if somebody woke me up in the middle of the night and slapped me across the face I'd still say Stephen Col-BEAR. But if people don't like what I do on this show, I say, 'That's Stephen Col-BEAR, I'm Stephen Colbert.'"

Source: Quoted in Bryce Donovan. "Great Charlestonian? ... Or the Greatest Charlestonian? Stephen Colbert." *Post and Courier,* April 30, 2011. www.postandcourier .com/stories/?newsID=83674.

intellectuals, who were very devout. I was raised to believe that you could question the Church and still be Catholic."[4] Although they encouraged religious questioning, the Colbert family also had a deep respect for tradition. In a rare description of his upbringing in an interview for *Rolling Stone* magazine in 2009, Colbert recalled a boyhood tradition that has been carried on to the present day. He said that his family, now numbering over fifty people with nieces and nephews, does a procession through the house on Christmas Eve, lining up from youngest to oldest: "The youngest puts the baby Jesus in the manger on Christmas Eve and we sing 'Silent Night.' It's very traditional."[5]

Though Colbert does not speak often about his early life, he describes his large family of eleven children as very happy. In an interview with Deborah Solomon for the *New York Times*, he once remarked: "I was very loved. My sisters like to say that they are surprised that I learned to walk and that my legs didn't become vestigial because I got carried around by them so much."[6] He has sometimes said that his own devotion to his wife and two children is based on the closeness of his upbringing.

Humor was important in the Colbert family as well. He calls his boyhood home a "humorocracy, where the funniest person in the room is king."[7] Stephen was also exposed to the comedy routines of some of the best-known professional comedians of the 1960s and early 1970s. He often listened to comedy albums recorded by comics Bill Cosby and George Carlin. He also appreciated the humor of television variety show hosts such as Dean Martin.

"Nothing Made Any Sense"

The young Colbert's life changed abruptly when he was ten years old. On September 11, 1974, his father and two older brothers were killed in an Eastern Airlines plane that crashed in dense fog as it approached Charlotte, North Carolina. All seventy-two people on board were killed. "Nothing made any sense after my father and my brothers died. I kind of just shut off,"[8] Colbert says.

As a result of the tragedy, Stephen became somewhat alienated and detached. He remembers:

> After they died … nothing seemed that important to me. And so, I immediately had sort of a, I won't say a cynical detachment from the world. But I would certainly say I was detached from what was normal behavior of children around me. It didn't make much sense. None of it seemed very important.[9]

His surroundings changed, too. Soon his mother relocated the family from James Island to a more urban neighborhood in Charleston, where Stephen found it difficult to make new friends. As he later recalled: "I was not from downtown. I did not know the kids there. I love Charleston … . I just wasn't accepted by the kids."[10]

By this time, Colbert's older siblings had already left home or were leaving to attend college, so suddenly the big, bustling family was reduced to just two: Stephen and his mother. Colbert recalls: "The shades were down, and she wore a lot of black, and it was very quiet. She was a daily communicant, [took daily Communion from her priest] and many times I was too. It was a constant search for healing. My mother gave that gift to all of us. I am so blessed to have been the child at home with her."[11]

From Tragedy, A Sense of Humor

In his adult years Colbert has noted how these early hard times helped him to develop a sense of humor. It became his mission to make his mother laugh. He has argued that people's sense of humor can only be found once they experience great tragedy and lose their childhood happiness. Colbert claims that all comedians have experienced some sort of deep sadness that brought them to comedy in order to cope with it. In his opinion, the development of a comic worldview is deeply rooted in the experience of tragedy.

As he retreated into himself in seventh grade, Stephen began to gravitate toward more insular pastimes. He became an ardent fan of science fiction, especially J.R.R. Tolkien books. He loved

As a teenager, Colbert was an avid fan of the Dungeons and Dragons board game, with its intricate rules of play and interesting characters.

the game Dungeons and Dragons. He could play it "every day, if I could find someone to play with me. If I couldn't find someone to play with me, I would work on my player character."[12] He played the game incessantly for four years.

Stephen loved the game for many reasons. He enjoyed developing and being consumed by his character, because it allowed him to escape the boredom of teen life and become something larger than life, someone who was adventurous and heroic. He claims that this role-playing was his early entry into acting. The game's complexity gave him a set of arcane rules and constructs that he had to abide by, yet still allowed him to develop his own character's responses to these predetermined situations. This early infatuation with a fantasy game is what Colbert believes to be the heart of improvisation. Though he did not know it as a child, in later years Colbert has argued that the game is the ideal training ground for acting and especially improvisation.

Breaking Out of His Shell

As a teenager, Stephen went to Charleston's Episcopal Porter-Gaud School, where he acted in some school plays, but did not excel in academics. At one point he wanted to study marine biology, but severe inner ear damage related to complications following surgery to repair a ruptured eardrum ruined these hopes. He was

Losing His Southern Accent

At a young age, Stephen Colbert noticed that Southerners with thick accents were often portrayed in popular culture as intellectually inferior to those without accents. Colbert describes why, despite growing up in the South, he has no discernible accent:

> At a very young age, I decided I was not gonna have a southern accent. Because people, when I was a kid watching TV, if you wanted to use a shorthand that someone was stupid, you gave the character a southern accent. And that's not true. Southern people are not stupid. But I didn't wanna seem stupid. I wanted to seem smart. And so I thought, 'Well, you can't tell where newsmen are from.'

Source: Quoted in Daniel Schorn. "The Colbert Report." CBS News, April 27, 2006. www.cbsnews.com/stories/2006/04/27/60minutes/main1553506.shtml?tag=content Main;contentBody.

left deaf in his right ear, and could no longer fulfill the primary requirement for a marine biologist—the ability to SCUBA dive (damaged ears make divers unable to equalize the pressure that builds up in the ears during a dive).

By the end of high school he started to become more social. He dabbled in poetry and recalls writing humorous things for friends: "There was this girl I had a crush on, and she had a teacher she didn't like at school. I had a real crush on her, so almost every day I would write her a little short story where she would kill him [the teacher] in a different way. But in sort of a James Bond-ian kind of explosives in the gas tank of his car kind of way."[13] When he found he could tell jokes and make others laugh, he became even more popular. In one year, from his junior to senior year, he went from being completely unknown to being voted the wittiest in his class. As he gained in popularity, he made more friends and was invited to more parties.

Conservative College

After high school graduation in 1982, Stephen enrolled in the all-male Hampden-Sydney College in central Virginia. The school's curriculum grounded him in the classics. Colbert says that his two years at Hampden-Sydney taught him to be more disciplined in his academic life. "It was a 'playtime's over' kind of place," he says. "I worked very hard. … I didn't have the self-discipline, so it took a lot more time to do the work. … You had to finish classes, come back to your room, and immediately start working."[14]

Hampden-Sydney was very old-fashioned and conservative. Colbert describes it as going to school over one hundred years ago. He took classes in rhetoric (discourse or speech), read the great books, studied Western civilization, and was expected to adhere to the school's strict honor code. As Colbert says, it was a "very regimented curriculum, and a 19th century emphasis on rhetoric and grammar—and all male."[15] Hampden-Sydney was where Stephen began to take performing seriously. His theater professor, Steve Coy, encouraged him. The professor's personality struck a chord with Colbert, because Coy was more open to unconventional ideas.

During this period, Stephen performed in the farce *Oh Dad, Poor Dad, Momma's Hung You in the Closet and I'm Feelin' So Sad*, by New York playwright Arthur Kopit. The play's plot involves a woman vacationing in a Caribbean resort with her son and dead husband, whose body she brings along in a casket and whose voice serves as the narrator. Stephen loved the dark theme of the play and especially the absurdity of the dialogue. He was impressed that the actors could say interesting things in the play, but say them in such a way as to make the audience laugh.

Discovering Theater

In 1984, after two years at Hampden-Sydney, Stephen transferred to Northwestern University in Chicago to major in theater. There he enjoyed a much more liberal environment. Colbert attributes wanting to change colleges to an even more serious desire to perform. He decided that theater was his passion and the only thing he was interested in studying.

In 1984, Colbert enrolled at Northwestern University in Evanston, Illinois, as a theater major.

Stephen initially planned to pursue a dramatic acting career. He studied the great plays, including the works of Shakespeare and George Bernard Shaw, for that purpose. He once said, "I meant to be a serious actor with a beard who wore a lot of black and wanted to share his misery with you."[16]

The program at Northwestern was very intense. Stephen's theater training included classes in other performing arts, such as dance, as well as working on theater productions in set design and as a member of the production crew. His academic requirements included courses in the history of theater, history of costume and décor, and drama criticism. The days were long; he often worked from early morning until late at night. Colbert recalls that his fellow students were just as dedicated as he was. It was the first time that he was immersed in an environment where everyone was equally devoted to theater.

The Birth of the "High-Status Idiot"

During the next couple of years at Northwestern, Stephen discovered a love of improvisational comedy. Just as important, he started to develop the "high-status idiot" character that would one day make him famous.

A number of former classmates at Northwestern trace the genesis of the ridiculous but lovable fake news character that Colbert eventually became known for back to specific roles performed during his Northwestern years. For example, in the school's production of *Terry Won't Talk*, Stephen played the role of a high school principal. According to playwright and director Aaron Posner, one of Colbert's classmates at Northwestern, the character played by Stephen was "very much a cigar-chomping, blue-blazered, high-status idiot. ....[Stephen] could play fairly reprehensible people in a way that you still really liked them."[17]

In another example, Stephen and a group of classmates and other colleagues formed the Journeymen Theater Ensemble. This troop performed *Rumpelstiltskin v. the Queen* and other plays at schools in the surrounding county. In the *Rumpelstiltskin* production, Stephen played the role of the miller. Classmates assert that Colbert's famous "high-status idiot" character is particularly reminiscent of this role played by the young Colbert because Colbert's miller was pompous and overblown.

Improvisational Comedy

Even though he loved formal theater, Stephen soon discovered a love of improvisational comedy after watching improv teams at a comedy club in Chicago. In improvisation, actors often come up with an idea for a scene and characters within it, but all dialogue is made up on the spot. Colbert recalls how he felt compelled to participate in this form of comedy: "I just loved going onstage with nothing planned."[18] Soon after, Stephen began performing with Northwestern's improv team, which was called the No Fun Mud Piranhas. He also performed comedy at IO, formerly ImprovOlympic, at Chicago's Annoyance Theater. Many up-and-coming comedians also did improv at IO, including Mike Myers, Chris Farley, and Tina Fey.

Colbert and Steve Carell enjoy an party following the Emmy Awards ceremony in 2006. Early in their careers, Colbert served as Carell's understudy in productions by Chicago's Second City comedy troupe.

Colbert at Home

Today, Colbert lives in New Jersey with his wife, Evelyn McGee-Colbert, and their three children, Madeline, Peter, and John. The couple first met in 1990. At the time, Colbert had a steady girlfriend who was pressing him to get married. Colbert returned to his hometown of Charleston to contemplate this important decision. That night, his mother took him to a show, where he met McGee. Colbert describes this first meeting as love at first sight: "I'll never forget it. I walk in and I see this woman across the lobby and I thought, 'That one. Right there.' At that moment, I thought, 'That's crazy. You're crazy, Colbert.' And it turned out I was right." His mother recalls that he spent the entire evening talking to her.

Colbert and his wife, Evelyn McGee-Colbert, right, have three children.

Colbert is a doting father. He has stated in the past that he only rarely allowed his three children to watch his show: "I say things in a very flat manner that I don't believe, and I don't want them to perceive Daddy as insincere. I basically tell them I'm professionally ridiculous."

Sources: Quoted in Bryce Donovan. "Great Charlestonian? ... Or the Greatest Charlestonian? Stephen Colbert." *Post and Courier,* April 30, 2006. www.postandcourier.com/stories/?newsID=83674.

Quoted in Marc Peyser. "The Truthiness Teller." *Newsweek,* February 12, 2006. www.newsweek.com/2006/02/12/the-truthiness-teller.html.

As his improv career took root, he started to relinquish his dream of serious, dramatic acting, dedicating himself instead to improv. As friend who performed with Colbert put it: "Speaking somebody else's words wasn't as exciting for him as creating on the fly on his own."[19]

Colbert completed Northwestern's three-year theater program in two years. After he graduated in 1986, he took a job at the box office at Second City, a comedy school and performance nightclub in Chicago. The school and club are famous for premiering comics who go on to become huge stars. Because he was employed there, Colbert was able to take improvisation classes at Second City's training center for free. He auditioned to perform with Second City's touring company, and was hired on the same day as several other budding comedians, including Amy Sedaris, Paul Dinello, Scott Allman, and Chris Farley. Colbert was thrilled. Among his talented colleagues was the young comedic actor Steve Carell. Colbert was Carell's understudy—in Second City terms, the guy who took Carell's place when Carell was out of town, not someone actually studying to play a part the way Carell did.

Colbert later described a particular moment onstage at Second City that made his transition from drama to comedy complete:

I saw someone fail onstage—terribly, *massively* fail onstage. And we backstage laughed so hard at this woman's failure, and our laughter was so joyful and not derisive. … And I thought, "This is healthier than straight theater." Because in straight theater when someone fails, you come backstage, and people are very quietly sort of touching up their makeup, going, "How's it going out there? It seems pretty quiet."…That is the moment when I said, "I will do this and not drama, I will do comedy and not drama," and never turned back.[20]

From the Stage to the Screen

At the end of his stint at Second City, in the early 1990s, Colbert moved to New York, along with Sedaris and Dinello, to develop *Exit 57*, a television comedy series that debuted on Comedy Central in 1995. Although the show was canceled after only twelve episodes, it received good reviews and was nominated for several CableACE awards in the categories of best writing, performance, and comedy series. Colbert recalls that budgets were extremely tight on the short-lived show: the actors would think up great sketches, but might not be able afford the necessary props. Colbert gives an example: "'Well, here's an idea,' he says of how development for the show would go. 'A guy gets woken up by a jackhammer. The jackhammer operator … ' and our producers would say, 'First of all, before you go any further—do you have a jackhammer? Because I don't have a jackhammer.'"[21]

Colbert went on to work with Steve Carell and others as a cast member and writer on the ABC comedy sketch show *The Dana Carvey Show,* a vehicle for *Saturday Night Live* star Dana Carvey that was canceled after only seven episodes. Sponsors pulled out after the show was described as being of questionable taste. After another failure to secure permanent work, Colbert worried that paying his bills would become a struggle. He had married and had one small child at the time, and he needed to think seriously about how to support his young family.

So Colbert took work wherever he could find it, writing bits for other shows, including *Saturday Night Live*. Working with *SNL* comedian Robert Smigel, with whom Colbert had worked on *The Dana Carvey Show*, Colbert cowrote and coproduced the recurring *SNL* cartoon "The Ambiguously Gay Duo" and other "TV Funhouse" cartoons for *SNL*. Colbert began to develop character voices while working on these cartoons, playing the voice of Ace, opposite Steve Carell as Gary.

To pay the bills, Colbert also took a job filming humorous segments for the ABC morning news and talk show *Good Morning America*. Although it was paid work, something he desperately needed at the time, he did not enjoy the restrictions of the format. Although only one episode ever aired, his stint at *Good Morning America* captured the attention of Madeline Smithberg, who was at that time the producer of a comedy show called *The Daily Show.*

Strangers with Candy

Around the same time, Colbert teamed up once again with fellow comedians Amy Sedaris and Paul Dinello. The trio developed the Comedy Central series *Strangers with Candy*, which would

Colbert, right, appears with Amy Sedaris in the 2005 feature film Strangers with Candy, *which was originally a television series on the Comedy Central cable network.*

go on to become a cult classic. The show was meant to parody afterschool specials. These specials, more like soap operas for the teen set, usually took place in a school setting and featured teen characters in trouble. *Strangers with Candy* told the story of forty-six-year-old high school dropout Jerri Blank, who returns to finish school after more than thirty years of homelessness and drug addiction.

Colbert played Chuck Noblet, a strict but uninformed history teacher who delivers questionable—and often absurd—moral lessons to his students. In one episode, for example, Noblet, in a strict, deadpan voice, tells his students: "The tragic irony of the Trojan War is that, though it was fought over Helen, who was young and beautiful, by the time they rescued her 10 years later, she was old and ugly."[22] A recurring joke in the series is that the married Noblet, who is carrying on a homosexual affair with another teacher, is completely oblivious to the fact that his sexual proclivities are readily apparent to everyone.

Strangers with Candy aired on Comedy Central in 1999 and 2000. Although it did not receive stellar reviews, it attracted a dedicated fan base. Colbert, in conjunction with Sedaris and Dinello, resurrected *Strangers with Candy* in a full-length film adaptation, which premiered at the Sundance Film Festival in 2005.

Although his many comedic writing and acting jobs had not yet led to a long-term commitment, Colbert was perfecting his humor, improvisational skills, and character-driven comedy. He was poised for the next phase in his career, and the one that would make him the most loved and well-known to audiences. Smithberg, the producer who had seen Colbert's *Good Morning America* work, had hired Colbert as a writer for *The Daily Show* in 1997. At the time, Colbert thought it would be much the same type of writing he did at *Good Morning America*, and did not see much future in the opportunity. Ironically, it would become one of the most important jobs in his career.

Chapter 2

The Daily Show Years

Whe hen Stephen Colbert was hired on the television comedy series *The Daily Show* in 1997 as a writer and performer, it changed his life in many ways. He would perfect a fake newsman persona and take his career in a new, more permanent direction. *The Daily Show* took Colbert from worrying about not being able to support his wife and child and doubting his choice of career to earning awards, fame, and the respect of his peers.

Colbert's Role on *The Daily Show*

The Daily Show is a late night satirical news program that airs on Comedy Central. When the show premiered in 1996, it was hosted by former sports commentator Craig Kilborn. Comedian Jon Stewart took over as host in January 1999. Initially, Colbert was not impressed with the new opportunity. He thought the show relied too much on small, unrelated skits to get laughs. He also did not like the infighting among the show's producers. In short, he says, "I did not believe in the show, I did not watch the show, and they paid dirt. It was literally just sort of—it was a paycheck to show up."[23]

With Stewart as host, the show, which originally focused on pop culture, took on a decidedly political tone, satirizing news stories, political leaders, and, most pointedly, media coverage of news and current events. The format of the show is very

Jon Stewart hosts an episode of The Daily Show, *which he joined in 1999. Colbert became a part of the show two years earlier as a writer and performer.*

consistent: Stewart opens with a monologue that offers a satirical take on the day's news stories and issues. Next is a segment that features an exchange with a "correspondent," played by one of several comedians who impersonate television news reporters and analysts. The correspondents usually sit at Stewart's anchor desk or pretend to report from another location, usually a live shot filmed in front of a green screen. The correspondents, often credentialed as some sort of "senior specialist," present patently ridiculous or exaggerated takes on current events while Stewart, as straight man, asks a host of probing questions.

Developing His Faux News Correspondent Character

Colbert wrote material for the show as well as played a news correspondent. While Stewart hosts *The Daily Show* as himself, Colbert, like all of the other correspondents, worked in character. Colbert developed a right-wing political pundit character

Colbert poses with television news personality Stone Phillips in 2006. Colbert modeled his correspondent character on The Daily Show *after Stone's on-screen style.*

that mocked the vanity of self-obsessed political correspondents. Colbert modeled himself after many media personalities, but in particular was inspired by Stone Phillips, an anchorman who hosted *Dateline NBC,* and news anchor Geraldo Rivera, who is best known for his flamboyant style:

> My natural inclination was Stone Phillips, who has the greatest neck in journalism. And he's got the most amazingly severe head tilt at the end of tragic statements … and then I also used Geraldo Rivera, because he's got this great sense of mission. He just thinks he's gonna change the world with this report. He's got that early seventies hip trench coat "busting this thing wide open" look going on.[24]

As Colbert developed the character, he also added the attributes of right-wing cable news pundit Bill O'Reilly, who hosts *The O'Reilly Factor* on Fox News Network. Colbert also parodies Glenn Beck, Sean Hannity, and other right-wing conservative personalities. These real-life news stars are known for taking events and editorializing them, usually bringing a "fear factor" to the news in which they tell their audience why they should be afraid of what is going on in the world, using their own interpretations of news events.

This sowing of fear and the air of self-importance and infallibility of many of these commentators are the key features of Colbert's invented persona. Colbert's character harks back to early roles in which he enjoyed playing characters who were able to say absurd things. He has referred to this character as "a fool who has spent a lot of his life playing not the fool."[25] He often uses this same technique when he interviews real experts for his otherwise fake news report. Colbert sometimes likes to just come out of nowhere with comments that fluster and flabbergast his interviewee:

> On *The Daily Show*, I'm essentially a very high status character, but my weakness is that I'm stupid. … I'll go into an interview with a guy who runs a Beatles museum for instance, for *The Daily Show*, and I'll confess to him that

I don't know who The Beatles are. Like, I mean, obviously I know who they are, I just don't know—like, "What was their big hit? I know obviously they had more than one big hit, but what was that big one? The one they always whistled?" I don't mind seeming like a fool.[26]

Playing the Fool

Originally one of four fake correspondents who filmed segments in studio or from remote locations, Colbert would frequently travel to different venues to file absurdly exaggerated reports on current news stories and conduct interviews with people related to the issue at hand. While the topics varied widely according to what news was making headlines, these reports typically poked as much fun at those who cover the news as at the news itself, even lambasting the entire genre of television news. Whatever the issue, Colbert's character spouts absurdities with what has now become his trademark stone face and self-important smirk.

Colbert describes one of his favorite faux-news-correspondent segments and how it exposed the absurdity of broadcast news journalism. In a piece called "Death and Taxes," Colbert went to Saratoga Springs, New York, because a computer glitch caused an X to be placed in the wrong box on all of the county employees' annual tax forms. All of the tax forms were printed with the X mark indicating that the three hundred employees were deceased. Colbert covered it in a unique way:

> We covered it as if there had been a disaster, three hundred people had died. … The reporter gets there and it is not what he thought it was but he won't let it go. He cannot let go the idea of this tragedy and that the people there are filled with rage, and I actually eventually got people to say that they were sad and that they were filled with rage. And it was a great triumph for me as a fake reporter to get them to buy into my idiocy.[27]

The Colbert character willingly humiliates himself for a laugh, to play the fool. Often, this means taking a legitimate social issue,

Bill O'Reilly

Colbert has used news personality Bill O'Reilly as a template for his character on *The Colbert Report.* O'Reilly is a best-selling author, syndicated columnist, and host of the political commentary program *The O'Reilly Factor* on Fox News Channel. Since its debut in 1996, *The Factor*

Colbert, right, appears with Fox News commentator Bill O'Reilly on the set of The O'Reilly Factor in 2007.

has gained a wide following and is one of the highest rated cable news shows on American television today. O'Reilly is one of the most powerful conservative forces in the media, although O'Reilly himself claims he does not embrace a strict conservative ideology and is registered as an independent.

Famous for his contentious style, O'Reilly brashly confronts those who oppose him. In one notorious encounter, O'Reilly shouted down Al Franken, who had written a book claiming that O'Reilly had misrepresented himself on numerous occasions; during the encounter, O'Reilly told Franken to "shut up," an exchange that was widely publicized. O'Reilly also engages in heated arguments regarding what he calls a "culture war" between those who embrace traditional values and those want to change America. The strong opinions expressed by O'Reilly and other conservative pundits provide much of the fodder for *The Colbert Report,* described by Colbert as "personality driven news. … It's what the host thinks about the story as much as the story itself."

Source: Quoted in David Cote. "As He Prepares to Move On from *The Daily Show,* the Host of the Upcoming *Colbert Report* Gets His Ulysses On." *Time Out New York,* June 9–15, 2005. http://newyork.timeout.com/arts-culture/651563/joyce-words.

such as discrimination, to absurd extremes. For example, in one clip, Colbert satirizes bigotry and discrimination when he interviews people who say they are discriminated against because of the colors of their tattooed skin, saying they are forced to live separate but unequal lives reminiscent of African Americans during the civil rights era. As part of the segment, Colbert interviews an African American man behind a civil ordinance banning tattoo parlors near public schools or churches. In his usual unflappable style, Colbert audaciously implies that the black man is discriminating against "people of color," or those who have chosen to tattoo their skin.

In another show, Colbert questions a smoker who says she suffers discrimination similar to Rosa Parks; Colbert, in characteristic deadpan, ends the clip with a parody of the "I Have a Dream" speech given by civil rights leader Martin Luther King, Jr. Colbert proclaims that he has a dream that "one day we will all be judged by the content of our character and not the color of our lungs."[28]

The Perfect Job

In some interviews, Colbert's deadpan demeanor was enough to allow the joke to evolve on its own. In one episode, a rancher in Washington was told he could not develop his property because it was home to many endangered species, including Bigfoot. While the rancher, Jim Baum, railed at the absurdity of putting the mythical Bigfoot on the list, Colbert's interview with a Bigfoot expert topped the gag. The expert likewise said that it was absurd to put Bigfoot on the list, not because the creature was mythical, but because Bigfoot was alive and well, and not endangered.

The Daily Show's humor works, in large part, because it so clearly echoes what goes on in real TV news shows. Many news shows *are* more about newspeoples' personalities than the news; many news stories *are* inflated or trivialized by correspondents who do not always have a good grasp of the subject. Although everything seems to be fodder for Stewart and his colleagues' mockery, *The Daily Show* does self-censor. When asked in an

A Practicing Catholic

Stephen Colbert is a devout Catholic. Although he does not always follow strict religious doctrine, his faith is a very important part of his life:

> I am highly variable in my devotion. From a doctrinal point of view or a dogmatic point of view or a strictly Catholic adherent point of view, I'm first to say that I talk a good game, but I don't know how good I am about it in practice. I saw how my mother's faith was very valuable to her and valuable to my brothers and sisters, and I'm moved by the words of Christ, and I'll leave it at that.

Although Colbert does not divulge many details about his personal life, including those that pertain to his faith, he does attend church regularly and even teaches Sunday school. About working with his young pupils, Colbert says, "I get to actually talk to someone who will take me seriously when I talk about religion—albeit I have to find somebody who's seven to take me seriously."

Sources: Quoted in Neil Strauss. "Stephen Colbert on Deconstructing the News, Religion, and the Colbert Nation." *Rolling Stone,* September 2, 2009. www.rollingstone.com/culture/news/stephen-colbert-on-deconstructing-the-news-religion-and-the-colbert-nation-20090902.

Quoted in Steven Daly. "The Second Most Powerful Idiot in America." *Telegraph,* May 18, 2008. www.telegraph.co.uk/culture/tvandradio/3673509/Stephen-Colbert-the-second-most-powerful-idiot-in-America.html.

interview if there were any topics that were off limits on *The Daily Show,* Colbert replied:

Well, obviously real tragedy, like the [July 7, 2005] London bombing, is off limits. No one wants to do comedy about that. But I would say there's almost nothing that can't be mocked on a certain level as long as it doesn't involve loss of life or deep human tragedy. I don't think we ever looked at something and said that's too ridiculous to make more ridiculous. Contrary to what people may say, there's no upper limit to stupidity. We can make everything stupider.[29]

His time at the *Daily Show* helped Colbert gain a deeper respect for the genre of political satire. Colbert recalls that although he was not particularly political before joining *The Daily Show*, eventually Stewart "infected me with his spirit of satire. I learned to talk passionately about things you care about and be fair to a position that you don't agree with. I realized that I had stumbled into a perfect job for me."[30]

Writing for *The Daily Show*

Colbert's correspondent performance was only part of what he contributed to the show. He also wrote a lot of the show's other content. In fact, Colbert and his fellow writers won three Emmys

Colbert, left, poses with costars Rob Corddry, Jon Stewart, Ed Helms, and Samantha Bee after the Emmy Awards ceremony in 2005. Colbert and his fellow writers won several Emmys for their work on The Daily Show.

for Outstanding Writing for *The Daily Show,* in 2004, 2005, and 2006. Colbert recounts this as an especially good time for him. He loved writing stories through the lens of his newsman character and coming up with specific stories that lent themselves to spoofing. The format—a nightly, topical show driven by the day's headlines—demanded a lot of material produced quickly. This allowed Colbert to become less attached to his material. As he explained, "It [the show] has got to be written by three, and the story just broke this morning. So, you can't be like egotistical about it and be precious about your words."[31]

Recurring Segments

Colbert was also able to continue his collaboration with Steve Carell, who was also a correspondent on *The Daily Show*. Colbert and Carell performed a segment called "Even Stevphen," a mock debate that examined political and cultural events. The segment's name is a composite of the comedians' first names, Stephen and Steven, but also emphasizes the similarities between the two. The duo would take on an issue to debate but usually ended up unleashing a chain of insults at one another, which often resulted in one or the other breaking down in tears. In an episode that aired in October 2000, for example, the senior pundit team pokes fun at certain Halloween rituals. In one somewhat poignant exchange, Carell teaches Colbert how to trick or treat as Colbert stages a mock breakdown because he was not allowed this rite of passage as a child.

In another episode, Carell and Colbert debate Islam versus Christianity, during which both comedians come off as the mindless zealots that they are satirizing. To settle their debate about which god is the one true god, the two challenge each other to a "pray-off" to see who would be struck down first—Carell as he prays to Allah or Colbert as he prays to the Christian god. During this, Jon Stewart (who is Jewish) interrupts them to say that the skit is going on too long. The two then conclude that they can be in agreement about one thing—both of their religions do not think too highly of Jews. They conclude that the two religions may not be so different after all.

Colbert's other important recurring segment on the *Daily Show* was "This Week in God," which featured Colbert's humorous take on religious topics in the news. In this skit, a "God Machine," a large black post with a red button, generated topics for discussion (such as "pharmaceutical Christianity," "Burger King Muslim," and "lesbian Methodism"). By pushing the button, Colbert would activate the God Machine, which would then flash religious imagery while making a "beepboopboop" sound (actually, a recording of Colbert's voice) before slowing down and landing on a particular image that represented the topic to be examined in the segment.

Colbert's reports ranged from lighthearted to the subversively provocative. One segment featured a French Burger King that caters to Muslims by serving meat that is prepared in accordance with Islamic dietary laws, and then poked fun of the health risks posed by fat-laden hamburger meat in general. Other segments poked fun at baptism, tithing, and other practices of Catholicism and many other religious traditions. Colbert's "This Week in God," segment, which he performed from 2003 to 2005, won him a wide following and made the "God Machine" famous as an icon for the comedic—and usually irreverent—examination of religious issues.

From Obscurity to Fame: The Presidential Election Coverage

The Daily Show's coverage of national and global political events and issues, though exaggerated for comical effect, usually has a serious point to make: exposing politicians' flawed or illogical arguments or weaknesses in media reporting, for example. Notable segments include former President George W. Bush's war on terror and the occupation of Iraq (dubbed "Mess-o-potamia").

It was the 2000 and 2004 presidential election campaigns, however, that rocketed the show's ratings—and Colbert's popularity—upward. In July 2000, Colbert and other cast members traveled to Philadelphia to file reports from the floor of the Republican National Convention as part of the show's award-winning "Indecision 2000"

Colbert mans the anchor desk during The Daily Show's *special "Indecision 2004" election-night coverage.*

coverage. Two weeks later, the show headed to Los Angeles for the Democratic National Convention. The show used the ongoing headline "Indecision 2004" in its coverage of the election four years later, too.

The show averaged more than 1.4 million viewers per episode. Covering a convention by poking fun at it seemed to appeal to many Americans, who tuned in, in many cases, instead of watching the real news shows. Colbert describes why political conventions are good fodder for comedy: "They're sales rallies where politicians say things people have already heard to people who already believe them."[32]

The effect of *The Daily Show* on the public is debated. Some complain it misinforms viewers, because many tune in for the jokes and satire instead of reading or listening to real news. Others argue *The Daily Show* is actually an important source of news: a 2007 study by the Pew Research Center, for example, found *Daily Show* viewers to be more informed than audiences of news shows on Fox, CNN, or National Public Radio. The Pew Research Center determined that 54 percent of *Daily Show* viewers had a high level of knowledge about current events and political subjects—the highest score recorded.

Colbert does not believe that *The Daily Show,* nor his involvement in it, amounts to this kind of responsibility. He thinks the audience is already informed about world events, which is why they find the show's material funny: "I think you have to have some handle on what's happening in the world to get our jokes."[33]

Colbert goes further to say that though he sometimes wishes he could influence people's political philosophies, he does not believe he can or does. What he does is pure entertainment. Colbert thinks that since most news shows are built on stories that enhance people's fear and apprehension, shows like *The Daily Show* are watched as an antidote to the real news: "I wish we had an effect on the way people think about politics, but I don't think we do. I see the show as a relief from the political process, especially now, when so much of politics is built on the idea of fear. We're falling down and going boom on camera."[34]

The Colbert Report Is Born

Since its debut, *The Daily Show* has launched many of its correspondents into independent careers. As Ben Karlin, the executive producer of the show, once said, "We don't have illusions about this show being the final stop for anyone. This is training ground."[35] Early on, Stephen Colbert and Steve Carell were identified as talented comedians with serious breakout potential. When Steve Carell started getting offers from other networks, he left Comedy Central, going on to star on NBC's hit comedy series *The Office.*

Colbert, too, needed a new opportunity. After six years perfecting his character on *The Daily Show*, Jon Stewart, along with Colbert and Ben Karlin, conceived the idea of creating a spin-off of *The Daily Show.* As Stewart said: "Stephen has such encyclopedic knowledge and I figured using himself as the foundation of a character like that, there was no question he could do this every day. He was just ready."[36] The trio reportedly referred to the new show as their version of the conservative news show *The O'Reilly Factor* with Stephen Colbert. Comedy Central—not wanting to lose Colbert to another network—bought the idea and agreed to run *The Colbert Report* for eight episodes in 2005. It would go on to become one of Comedy Central's highest rated series, and Colbert would become a force in his own right.

Chapter 3

The Colbert Report

As a Second City troupe member and as an actor and writer on *The Daily Show*, Stephen Colbert had always been part of an ensemble. But his new show, *The Colbert Report,* launched on October 17, 2005, featured just him. This new step was a big leap in responsibility, as Colbert was fully in charge of all of the material for the show as well as its sole star.

Becoming a Host and Leader

In interviews before the show aired, critics asked Colbert whether he thought the American public would be interested in a show devoted entirely to his *Daily Show* character. On the *Daily Show*, Colbert's character was entertaining, but was clearly a secondary, supporting figure—just one of several people who made the show work. Whether Colbert could sustain a show on his own, or become a star in his own right, was unproven.

Yet questions about the show's success were quickly answered the first week it aired, when 1 million viewers tuned in. Years later, the show continues to draw an average nightly audience of 1.2 million viewers each night.

While *The Daily Show* is news parody, *The Colbert Report* is more about the cult of personality that characterizes many political opinion shows—the perfect vehicle for Colbert's deadpan humor and sharp commentary. Colbert's show focuses more on the news correspondent inserting himself into the news—what he thinks about it, why his opinion is important, and trumping up himself as a character, in much the

As the host of The Colbert Report, *Colbert earns laughs with an on-air persona that satirizes the egotism of many real-life political commentators.*

same way radio host Rush Limbaugh or news commentator Bill O'Reilly approach their shows. Colbert's character makes fun of these news hosts' egotism. Columnist Johnny Frohlichstein summed up the difference between *The Daily Show* and *The Colbert Report:* "The main difference between these partners in comedy is the essence of their shows. Stewart focuses more on day-to-day news while fusing outlandish comparisons with hard facts. However, *The Colbert Report* is a complete character

The Set of *The Colbert Report*

The Colbert Report is produced in a studio in New York City. The set, called "the Eagle's Nest," is reminiscent of the set for *The O'Reilly Factor.* A series of LED displays feature patriotic images, such as the Stars and Stripes and the Statue of Liberty. Colbert describes how the set was designed to amplify his status as host:

> Everything on the show has my name on it, every bit of the set. One of the things I said to the set designer ... was "One of your inspirations should be [DaVinci's painting] *The Last Supper.* All the architecture of that room points at Jesus' head, the entire room is a halo, and he doesn't have a halo." And I said, "On the set, I'd like the lines of the set to converge on my head." And so if you look at the design, it all does, it all points at my head. And even radial lines on the floor, and on my podium, and watermarks in the images behind me, and all the vertices, are right behind my head. So there's a sort of sun-god burst quality about the set around me. And I love that. That's status. We just try everything we can to pump up my status on the show.

Source: Quoted in Nathan Rabin. "Interview: Stephen Colbert." A.V. Club, January 25, 2006. www.avclub.com/articles/stephen-colbert,13970/.

satire that focuses on the particulars of Colbert's character, with the actual news coming second."[37]

As the show's lead, Colbert works long hours. The production schedule is punishing. Colbert creates and performs four new half-hour shows a week, about nine months a year. Colbert manages by taking it one show at a time, trying to make each show fresh, without letting the following shows, and the work involved in producing week by week, influence the one he currently works on. About the grueling demands of the job, Colbert remarks, "Early in the process I started calling this place 'the joy machine.' Because if it's not a joy machine, it's just a machine ... and then you get caught in the gears."[38] His work seems to have paid off. Colbert has developed such a loyal following that he calls them his "Colbert Nation."

A Satire of Conservative Punditry

Colbert imitates real life news personalities to define and enhance his character's development. Some critics note that the most recognizable show Colbert parodies is Bill O'Reilly's nightly news show *The O'Reilly Factor.* In a review in the *New Yorker*, Nancy Franklin comments that Colbert "resembles nobody more than he does Bill O'Reilly, and like O'Reilly, he conveys fake humility and easy rage toward inappropriate targets."[39] O'Reilly himself says he enjoys the parody, finding Colbert's imitation not mocking but rather lighthearted and affectionate, even flattering. O'Reilly argues, "The formula of his program is, they watch the 'Factor' and they seize upon certain themes that work for him. He ought to be sending me a check every week, 'cause we're basically the research for his writers. I feel it's a compliment."[40]

But Colbert has said that the show is far more than a simple parody of any single personality. He believes his show targets the current era in news coverage, in which the commentator has become the show. He sees this personality-driven aspect at work in many different arenas: "The show is not about O'Reilly. ... The show is about what is behind those things, which is: What I say is reality. And that never ends. Every politician is going to want to enforce that, or every person in Hollywood—every person."[41]

The Colbert Report's "Thesis Statement"

Colbert focuses on how the media has changed from reporting noteworthy events to becoming more about the newsmakers. His act, which includes inventing his own catchy witticisms and

Supreme Court nominee Harriet Miers, left, appears with President George W. Bush at the White House in 2005. Colbert has cited Bush's explanation as to why he nominated Miers for the post as an example of what he refers to as "truthiness."

vocabulary, has caught on with the media. For example, during the show's first episode, Colbert coined the word "truthiness"—which, with his character's typical anti-intellectual confidence, he defined as the truth one feels in the gut rather than what one can learn or know from books. As Colbert said during the episode: "Tonight's word: Truthiness. Now I'm sure some of the word-police, the 'wordinistas' over at Websters, are gonna say, 'Hey, that's not a word!' Well, anybody who knows me knows that I am no fan of dictionaries or reference books. They're elitist. Constantly telling us what is or isn't true, what did or didn't happen."[42]

Colbert's truthiness highlights an increasingly real phenomenon in American culture, in which politicians and commentators claim that their own assertions, even when based on exaggeration or their own opinion, are more accurate than the truth. Language columnist Mark Peters has aptly defined truthiness as "the degraded condition of truth in media, government, nonfiction, and elsewhere."[43]

The word was inspired, in part, by former president George W. Bush's tendency to play loose and free with vocabulary when speaking in public. Colbert used Bush's 2005 nomination of lawyer Harriet Miers to the Supreme Court in his explanation of "truthiness." At the time, many claimed that Miers, a former White House counsel with close personal ties to Bush, was unqualified for such a lofty position, largely because she had never been a judge and lacked a clear record on many of the issues pertinent to the Supreme Court. But as Colbert put it:

> We are divided between those who think with their head and those who *know* with their heart. Consider Harriet Miers. If you think about Harriet Miers, of course her nomination's absurd. But the president didn't say he thought about his selection … .He didn't have to. He feels the truth about Harriet Miers. And what about Iraq? If you think about it, maybe there are a few missing pieces to the rationale for war, but doesn't taking Saddam out *feel* like the right thing?[44]

At the end of the first episode, he further defined and defended his new concept in what would become his trademark deadpan mockery, claiming that while anyone could read the news, he was going to feel the news to the audience. Colbert has since called this the "thesis statement" for the show, and the word has come to exemplify the way American politicians redefine debates and the context of their comments. One year after the first episode aired,

Colbert said, "Language has always been important in politics, but language is incredibly important to the present political struggle. Because if you can establish an atmosphere in which information doesn't mean anything, then there is no objective reality. The first show we did … was our thesis statement: What you wish to be true is all that matters, regardless of the facts."[45]

The Importance of Truthiness

Truthiness continues to catch on in the news media and elsewhere, and represents a powerful and important concept—and by some accounts, problem—facing society. The *Merriam-Webster* dictionary, the American equivalent of the *Oxford English Dictionary*, recognized this in 2006, when it announced "truthiness" as its word of the year. As Merriam-Webster president John Morse said about this honor, "We're at a point where what constitutes truth is a question on a lot of people's minds, and truth has become up for grabs. 'Truthiness' is a playful way for us to think about a very important issue."[46]

Indeed, Colbert has used the concept of truthiness not only to mock but also to challenge Americans to think critically and examine reality, even as the media, the Internet, and technology lull them into doing otherwise. As critic Ethan Mills commented, "Through his brand of parody and satire, Stephen may be one of the greatest champions for the traditional values of truth and critical thinking on basic cable today. By relentlessly making fun of truthiness he can incite us to reflect on the direction of our culture, to question truthiness and those who wield it."[47]

Praise for the concept continued in 2006, when the American Dialect Society also called "truthiness" the word of the year. In 2010, the word appeared in the *New Oxford American Dictionary,* with Colbert named as its founder. The word continues to spread and has even spawned the trend of adding "–iness" to the end of words, such as describing Paris Hilton's celebrity as "fame-iness" or describing misinformed persons' ability to sound like they know what they're talking about as "referenciness." Because of this, Stanford linguist Arnold Zwicky has gone so far to call the suffix the "Colbert suffix."[48]

Awards and Honors

The kudos that Colbert has received over the years are evidence of the show's popularity and recognition of his status. In 2006, *Time* magazine named Colbert to its annual "TIME 100" list of the world's most influential people. The same year, *New York* magazine named Colbert, along with Jon Stewart, one of the dozen most influential persons in the media. Other media outlets have joined in, and in December 2007, the Associated Press named Colbert Celebrity of the Year.

Colbert poses with the prestigious Peabody Award, which was presented to his show in 2008.

The show's writing has also garnered critical acclaim. *The Colbert Report* received Emmy Awards for Outstanding Writing in 2008 and 2010. The show also received the Peabody Award for Excellence in Broadcasting in 2008. As he accepted his Peabody, Colbert said in his usual deadpan, "I proudly accept this award and begrudgingly forgive the Peabody Committee for taking three years to recognize greatness."

Other awards acknowledge the act. For example, in June 2008 the senior class of Princeton University presented its commencement speaker Colbert with "The Understandable Vanity Award," which consisted of a drawing and a mirror. Gazing into the mirror, Colbert raved in mock arrogance: "I've never seen anything more beautiful."

Source: Quoted in Reuters. "Comedy Central's 'The Colbert Report' Honored with Prestigious Peabody Award." April 2, 2008. www.reuters.com/article/2008/04/02/idUS203939+02-Apr-2008+PRN20080402.

Quoted in Jennifer Greenstein Altmann. "Seniors Celebrate Achievements and Share Laughs at Class Day." News at Princeton, June 2, 2008. www.princeton.edu/main/news/archive/S21/24/37A93/index.xml?section=featured.

Never Mean-Spirited

Playing a character grants Colbert the freedom to say things that would unnerve viewers had they come out of the mouth of a real newscaster, or even a sincere comedian. This is no accident: When Colbert, Stewart, and Karlin initially designed the show, Colbert said he had to come off as sympathetic. Stewart seconded the notion, arguing that Colbert's character could pull off this naïveté nicely because he is simply an idiot. Colbert says, "The audience wouldn't forgive Jon for saying things most comedians would want to say. But we can say almost anything, because it's coming out of the mouth of this character."[49]

Key to this accomplishment is the fact that Colbert never breaks character—he plays the smug, self-obsessed right-wing cable newscaster throughout each episode, no matter how outrageous his commentary. He usually makes his point by saying the exact opposite, keeping a poker face all the while. In one episode, for example, Colbert did a sketch about eating disorders, looking directly into the camera and saying, "Girls, if we can't see your

By playing a character on his show rather than himself, Colbert is able to deliver jokes that are outrageous or absurd as a way of making keen political points.

I Am America (And So Can You!)

Colbert's satirical book *I Am America (And So Can You!)*, a collaborative effort between Colbert and a host of Comedy Central writers, was published in 2007. It quickly rose to the number one spot on the *New York Times* best-seller list. As an extension of his fake news show, the book features Colbert, in his pundit persona, satirizing various aspects of American society, including religion, the media, education, and other topics. On the subject of child rearing, for example, Colbert offers the following advice: "Don't worry if a rule makes sense—the important thing is that it's a rule. Arbitrary rules teach kids discipline: If every rule made sense, they wouldn't be learning respect for authority, they'd be learning logic."

Colbert holds a copy of I Am America (And So Can You!), *which he cowrote with several writers from his show.*

In a chapter on class war, Colbert puts forth that "class distinctions aren't just used to figure out where you sleep on a cruise ship. They are also used by pollsters and advertisers to better understand our buying habits. If you know which class you belong to, you know which commercials you should pay attention to." As Colbert says about the absurd musings that make up *I Am America (And So Can You!)*: "You won't find these opinions in any textbook, unless it happens to be one I've defaced."

Source: Stephen Colbert. *I Am America (And So Can You!)*. New York: Grand Central Publishing, 2007, p, 11, 162, 194.

ribs, you're ugly."[50] The statement was over-the-top, yet somehow still was able to make the point that the universal condemnation of a health issue can come off as harsh and judgmental. The abrupt connection between the two is what makes the line humorous.

No group seems safe. Other examples of Colbert's starkly humorous takes on sacred topics include homosexuality ("There's nothing wrong with being gay. I have plenty of friends who are going to hell"), revered social icons ("I just think Rosa Parks was overrated. Last time I checked, she got famous for breaking the law"), and finally, knowledge in general ("I don't trust books; they're all fact, no heart").[51]

The Audience Plays Along

Colbert's humor also works in part because of his relationship with his audience. Colbert has commented that he considers his audience part of the show, so much so that his show has two characters—Colbert and the audience. "They're the other character," he says. "If they're not there, then I've got no friction. I've got no one to talk to."[52]

The audience not only gets Colbert's desire to make them a part of the show, they actively seek out chances to prove it. Before each show, Colbert asks the audience to shout "Stephen" as loud as they can. The audience always keeps it up until Colbert, in character, makes them stop. People wait in long lines outside the show hoping for a chance to become part of the audience.

The Wørd

Like many real news shows, Colbert's show has a set format that is followed fairly religiously every night. After the show's opening sequence, *The Colbert Report* typically begins with a fake news broadcast that features the week's events and top stories. A particular news item usually leads into the show's signature segment: "The Wørd." In "The Wørd," Colbert speaks out on a particular topic while satirical bullet points flash on a side screen. These usually undercut, contradict, or convey the true meaning of

Colbert's statements in some way; sometimes they just mock the host. In one segment, for example, Colbert claims that Africa has more elephants than it did ten years ago. The screen commentary reads "Babar getting busy." Colbert mentions that he doesn't know whether it is a fact that elephants are making a comeback, and the screen flashes, "It isn't."[53] The segment is a parody of Bill O'Reilly's "Talking Points" segment, in which O'Reilly talks while captions that sum up the heart of his ideas appear on the screen.

In an example from the February 28, 2011, episode, Colbert attacks the idea that the United States has to cut defense spending to improve the economy. He argues that, in fact, exporting weapons is what America does best. In defending the sale of fighter jets to other countries, Colbert says that the best part is that the jets are obsolete. The screen flashes "still runs on Windows 98." When Colbert contends that selling arms to our enemies is as "American as napalm pie," the screen flashes "Just like mom used to drop."[54] The satire of the commentary is enhanced with these tidbits, allowing the skit to become a sight gag as well.

Other Segments

"The Wørd" is often followed by a skit, usually one of the many recurring segments that have aired periodically through the years. In the humorously titled "Formidable Opponent," for example, Colbert debates a variety of topics with himself. The segment is filmed to appear as if two Stephen Colberts are facing each other, each wearing different colored ties. One of the characters argues Colbert's trademark ultraconservative viewpoint while the other offers a more liberal take on the issue at hand. Generally, the staunchly conservative Colbert wins the debate, usually by suggesting an outlandish scenario that could occur if the liberal Colbert has his way. For example, in one debate over immigration, the conservative Colbert warns that if the United States eases its immigration policies, the liberal Colbert could lose his anchorman position to an illegal alien named Esteban Colberto who hosts a program called *Colberto Reporto Gigante*.

A makeup artist prepares Colbert, right, for an interview with Arizona congressman Raul Grijalva for a recurring segment on The Colbert Report *titled "Better Know a District" in 2007.*

Another popular segment is "Better Know a District," in which Colbert interviews a member of Congress who represents a particular district in the House of Representatives. The interview is preceded by a humorous history lesson on the district. The interviews typically feature off-the-wall questions that seek to mock the representatives, catch them off guard, or otherwise insult or confuse them. For example, Colbert asked Donna Christensen, a Democrat who represents the U.S. Virgin Islands, "Isn't it time to drop the whole virgin act?" When the befuddled representative asked what else they would call themselves, Colbert responded, "Trollop Islands? The Been-Around-the-Block Islands? The Not-Until-the-Third Date Islands?"[55] In another memorable clip, Colbert revealed that Georgia Republican Lynn Westmoreland could not recite the Ten Commandments, even after the congressman spearheaded a campaign to have them displayed in both the House of Representatives and the Senate. The popularity of "Better Know a District" has inspired a number of spin-offs, including "Better Know a Founder," "Better Know a Candidate," and "Better Know a President."

Colbert used one "Better Know a Founder" skit to mock the reality fashion show *Project Runway* while making a point about Thomas Jefferson's affair with his slave Sally Hemings. Colbert gathered three Jefferson imitators in a competition he called "America's Top Jefferson." The skit opened with Tim Gunn, who has a prominent role in *Project Runway*, critiquing the three Jeffersons' costumes. Colbert next interviewed the three Jeffersons, asking them which accomplishment they would like to be known for: advocate of religious freedom, founder of the University of Virginia, writer of the Declaration of Independence, or "the guy who [had sex with] his slaves?"[56] The mock interviews continued, and Colbert ended by tossing a coin to crown America's top Jefferson.

Guest Interviews

No matter which segment is featured, the final third of *The Colbert Report* is almost always a guest interview. Colbert has no problem attracting guests from all walks of life. Just a few notables who have appeared on the show include NPR correspondent Eric Weiner, *New York Times* columnist Maureen Dowd, actress Jane Fonda, comedian Conan O'Brien, boxer Sugar Ray Leonard, comedian Steve Martin, artist William Wegman, Vice President Joe Biden, and former secretary of state Henry Kissinger.

Not surprisingly, most of the politicians, authors, and other celebrity guests get mildly ridiculed by Colbert. When he interviewed John Mica, Republican representative from Florida, for example, Colbert asked in a deep, serious voice whether Mica had to take off his toupee when he went through security. Most of Colbert's guests are in on the joke. As one reviewer says:

Colbert's character never bullies or shouts at his guests. "The emotion of the shouting would shut the guest down," [Colbert] observes. Perhaps it's this kinder, gentler approach that regularly leads to the remarkable sight of apparently sane guests getting sucked into the parallel universe of Colbert's

Colbert tapes an interview with Stuart Beck, Palau's ambassador to the United Nations, in 2006. Many famous politicians, journalists, actors, artists, and other high-profile personalities have appeared on Colbert's show.

famous neologism "truthiness," that is feelings-as-logic. On *The Colbert Report* one regularly sees real politicians getting so bamboozled that they can barely respond when Colbert blithely insists, 'I'm not making this up—I'm imagining it!' Or when he bellows forth the victorious non-sequiter, "I accept your apology!"[57]

Colbert says he does not ambush his guests: "Everybody knows what they're in for with me. I say exactly the same thing to everyone before the interview: 'I'm not an assassin. I do the show in character—and he's an idiot; he's willfully ignorant of everything we're going to talk about. Disabuse me of my ignorance. Don't let me put words in your mouth.'"[58]

Some of the interviews end up making significant political points. In one poignant interview, Colbert interviewed Daniel Ellsberg, who was responsible for leaking the Pentagon Papers to the mainstream media in 1971. At a time when the Vietnam War was becoming unpopular, the Pentagon Papers proved that the United States had illegally expanded the Vietnam War and that the government had deliberately misinformed the American people about various aspects of the war. At the time, Ellsberg was considered a traitor, and some even suggested he should be tried for treason. Ellsberg was the first man to be criminally prosecuted for a defense leak. Colbert used the interview to compare Ellsberg to Wikileaks founder Julian Assange, who in 2010 and 2011 leaked numerous secret government papers to the media. Through his interview with Ellsberg, Colbert was able to freely comment on the concept of free speech, and how it is only through the passage of time that Ellsberg is now a revered public figure in the fight for the protection of leaks as a First Amendment right.

Although Colbert works with a script—he writes much of his own material—he also improvises according to how his interviews play out. Indeed, ad-libbing much of the show is a chance to display his razor sharp wit. Colbert's former college roommate Eric Goodman, now a Disney executive, comments on Colbert's ability: "You wonder, 'How does Stephen do it?' He has to twist it in his head so he says something completely absurd, which he would never say in real life, but seems completely plausible."[59]

Hard to Lose the Character

Colbert has so thoroughly immersed himself in his on-air persona that, not surprisingly, he has to make a conscious effort to abandon it when he enters his home life. He has to make sure to leave behind not just the stress of the job but also his character when he comes home to his family. In an interview with *Vanity Fair,* he explained, "Letting go and not being the boss is much harder than letting go of my character … .That's why I drive myself home at night. … I drive home and I crank my tunes. And by the time I get there, I'm normal again."[60]

Chapter 4

Colbert Unleashed

Encouraged by the growing popularity of *The Colbert Report*, Colbert took his character in new directions. With the help of his fans, he became an influential voice not only in popular culture and the media but on the real political stage.

Ribbing the President

Colbert got his first chance to do this just six months after *The Colbert Report* debuted, in April 2006. He was asked to deliver the keynote speech at the annual White House Correspondents' Association dinner—an event that typically features a good-natured roast of the president. When Associated Press reporter Mark Smith booked Colbert for the event, he says, he knew little of the satirist's act, except that "he not only skewers politicians, he skewers those of us in the media."[61]

After opening remarks, Colbert stepped to the podium. With then-president George W. Bush sitting just one seat away, Colbert mercilessly lampooned Bush's policies on the Iraq War and other events. Completely in high-status idiot character, Colbert remarked with false admiration and a straight face, "He believes the same thing Wednesday that he believed on Monday, no matter what happened Tuesday. Events can change; this man's beliefs never will."[62] Colbert also mocked core Republican beliefs when he said, "I believe the government that governs best is the government that governs least. And by these standards, we have set up a fabulous government in Iraq."[63]

Colbert performs in character as the featured speaker at the annual White House Correspondents' Dinner in 2006. His controversial jokes gained him some negative attention in the media, but they caught on with Internet audiences and ultimately expanded his fan base.

Not content to lampoon only the president and his party, Colbert delivered a scathing critique of Washington's press corps, the very people who invited him to the event. He accused them of simply buying into the administration's reasons for supporting tax cuts, using weapons of mass destruction as a reason to invade Iraq, and minimizing global warming.

A Defining Moment

Overall, his performance was much more pointed than other comics had been at previous dinners, and afterward, almost everyone in the media had an opinion of it. Richard Cohen of the *Washington Post* called the comedian just plain rude. Chris Lehmann wrote in the *Observer* that the "act was the opposite

"The Room No Longer Matters"

Many reviews of Stephen Colbert's performance at the 2006 White House Correspondents' Association dinner were highly critical. Several inferred that the comedian bombed because he did not get many big laughs in the room. According to one reviewer, however, the reaction in the room no longer matters because Colbert's performance, like many important public events, was immediately posted on the Internet:

> Colbert wasn't playing to the room, I suspect, but to the wide audience of people who would later watch on the Internet. If anything, he was playing against the room—part of the frisson [thrill] of his performance was the discomfort he generated in the audience. ... To the audience that would watch Colbert on Comedy Central, the pained, uncomfortable, perhaps-a-little-scared-to-laugh reaction shots were not signs of failure. They were the money shots. They were the whole point. In other words, what anyone fails to get who said Colbert bombed because he didn't win over the room is: the room no longer matters. Not the way it used to. The room, which once would have received and filtered the ritual performance for the rest of us, is now just another subject to be dissected online.

Source: James Poniewozik. "Stephen Colbert and the Death of 'The Room.'" Tuning In, *Time*, May 3, 2006. unedin.blogs.time.com/2006/05/03/stephen_colbert_and_the_death/.

of ballsy confrontation … the material came off as shrill and airless."[64] Others, however, lauded the speech. *Time* TV critic James Poniewozik said that Colbert's points, though sometimes cringe-inducing, were right on target. *New York Times* columnist Frank Rich agreed, calling the speech "the defining moment of the 2006 [midterm election] campaign."[65]

Colbert defended his appearance, saying he was there to do jokes. He said his jokes were aimed not at the audience in the room, but rather at his television audience (the event was broadcast on C-SPAN). Indeed, Colbert was primarily playing to the millions of people who viewed the speech on the Internet. Amid the media buzz about Colbert's performance, the video of his speech went viral. Within two days of the event, 2.7 million people watched it on YouTube alone. As one observer noted: "[Colbert] was invited to give the keynote speech at a dinner for the president and wound up delivering a controversial, possibly very funny, possibly horribly unfunny, possibly bravely patriotic, and possibly near-seditious monologue that earned him a crazed mob of lunatic followers who await his every command."[66]

Colbert brought criticism of the president, as well as of the news media, directly to the public. He turned a relatively small, typically uncontroversial event into a national debate and invited the American public to participate. Colbert recognized that this was his target audience—and this tactic would be what would propel him to the forefront of political discourse. In this way, Colbert made the mainstream media irrelevant by going directly to the public. As Poniewozik said in *Time*, Colbert merely pointed out "how authority is fragmented and democratized in the Internet era." While in decades past the job of the media was to "assess and interpret for the masses,"[67] the Internet has made that function obsolete. Colbert and others like him realize that harnessing the Internet means harnessing public opinion.

The Colbert Nation

Colbert's stone-cold accurate imitation of blustering news punditry and hilarious commentary had already earned him a fan base among viewers who appreciated parody and political satire.

In 2006, Colbert's fans tallied more than 6.3 million votes in an online poll to have this bridge spanning the Danube River in Hungary named "The Stephen Colbert Bridge."

Following his razor sharp press corps speech, however, his popularity reached new heights. The Colbert Nation became a force in itself.

Colbert encourages his viewers not just to watch his show, but to become part of the joke and join in the game to influence the world. According to Colbert, he did not encourage his fans to behave as a bloc that supports the show—though Colbert's character often prefaces his remarks by addressing his audience presumptuously as "Nation," the group of devoted fans and supporters known as the Colbert Nation evolved on its own. As Colbert put it in a 2009 interview with *Rolling Stone*: "We invented the Colbert Nation, but then we discovered it was real. We didn't make it happen, they self-organized it. I love that relationship. We can't always have it, and you can't force that. You just have to acknowledge it."[68]

The Colbert Nation enthusiastically adopts causes taken up by Colbert, in or out of character. These sometimes stuntlike acts typically land him, his show, and his audience in the news. For example, Colbert once mentioned on the show that the Saginaw Spirit minor league hockey team was holding a name-our-mascot contest. Colbert asked his fans to bombard the team's website with votes for Steagle Colbeagle the Eagle—which subsequently won and became the team's mascot during the 2006–2007 season.

Similarly, in 2006 Colbert urged his followers to go to a website and vote in a poll to name a Hungarian bridge that crosses the Danube River "The Stephen Colbert Bridge." The comedian received more than 6.3 million votes—millions more than any other entry. The ambassador to Hungary, however, declared that according to Hungarian law, Colbert would have to be fluent in Hungarian and declined to have the bridge named after him.

His Fans Are Ready to Follow

Colbert has also used his show to mock Wikipedia, the online encyclopedia that anyone can edit. He often tells his audience to use it as a replacement for facts and books. To prove his thesis that truth is flexible and that if enough people believe something,

Short track speed skater Katherine Reutter wears a sponsorship patch with the logo of The Colbert Report *on the leg of her skating suit during a race in Montreal, Canada, in 2009.*

it becomes reality, Colbert once asked his followers to alter a Wikipedia page on elephants to say that the African elephant population had recently tripled. Scores of his fans obliged. In the end, Wikipedia locked down the page so that it could not be changed, but the prank demonstrated the willingness of the Nation to prove his point.

Another time, when the U.S. Olympic speed skating team lost its largest sponsor, Dutch bank DSB, Colbert turned to his Nation. Asking his fans to donate to the team so the show could become the new sponsor, Colbert exclaimed: "We must ensure that it is America's 38-inch thighs on that medal platform!"[69] Colbert signed a sponsorship agreement on November 2, 2009, during a show. In exchange for the sponsorship, the team's logo was changed to a Colbert Nation logo, which is stitched directly onto the skaters' suits.

Some of the things Colbert asks of his Nation are silly, prank-ish, and self-aggrandizing (such as seeing his name incorporated

Charitable Giving

Stephen Colbert is well known for his charitable activities. He has raised many thousands of dollars for a variety of causes, including Autism Speaks, a national organization that researches causes of and cures for autism; the Yellow Ribbon Fund, which assists injured service members and their families;

Colbert and Jimmy Fallon, right, perform an over-the-top version of Rebecca Black's "Friday" on Late Night with Jimmy Fallon.

and the Canadian support group Parkinson Society. Like all things associated with Colbert, these fund-raising events generally feature plenty of good-natured comedy.

In April 2011, Colbert appeared on the comedy show *Late Night with Jimmy Fallon* to sing "Friday." The song, written and performed by thirteen-year-old Rebecca Black, became a viral hit in 2011 with over 82 million views of Black's music video online. At the same time, it gained much negative attention after it received over 1.6 million "dislikes" from YouTube viewers. Colbert took it up because he thought the song's popularity would make his parody of it instantly recognizable. The musical extravaganza featured cheerleaders and appearances by the musical group the Roots and American Idol contestant Taylor Hicks. A reviewer for *Rolling Stone* wrote, "There's a lot to love in this clip, but the best thing about it is that everyone involved is celebrating the year's most absurd pop hit rather than making fun of the 13-year-old Black." The event raised over $50,000 for Donors Choose, a charity that donates classroom supplies to underfunded schools.

Source: Matthew Perpetua. "Stephen Colbert and Jimmy Fallon Perform Rebecca Black's 'Friday.'" *Rolling Stone,* April 4, 2011. www.rollingstone.com/culture/blogs/rolling-stone-video-blog/stephen-colbert-and-jimmy-fallon-perform-rebecca-blacks-friday-20110404.

into a mascot or logo); others are intended to demonstrate the power and awful awesomeness of groupthink (such as altering content). The effect of both is that Colbert, unlike any other comedian, has an army of followers who have made themselves available to play out his jokes in real time, in the real world. As Adam Sternbergh has observed in *New York* magazine, "[Colbert] now stands astride the political landscape, his mob of followers at the ready."[70]

Presidential Run

Colbert's infectious comedic personality and his ability to galva-nize his fans prompted him to launch a fake run for the presi-dency. A fake campaign was the perfect platform to send out his unflagging message—that American politics and politicians, as well as the news media's reporting of politics and politicians, border on a joke.

Colbert first hinted at a 2008 presidential run when he appeared on talk shows to promote his book, *I Am America (And So Can You!)*. On Larry King's CNN talk show on October 14, 2007, for example, he put forth the absurd proposition that he might possibly seek the nomination from both the Republican and Democratic parties, arguing that this demonstrated true cour-age because he could lose twice.

Before he had officially announced his candidacy, he also spoke to supporters as a guest contributor in Maureen Dowd's October 14 *New York Times* column, poking fun at the fact that most presidential candidates tend to be white, Christian males: "I know why you want me to run, and I hear your clamor. ... It's clear that the voters are desperate for a white, male, middle-aged Jesus-trumpeting alternative."[71]

On October 16, 2007, Colbert officially announced his cam-paign to run for president in South Carolina, his home state. With red, white, and blue balloons floating down on the set of his own show, Colbert proclaimed, "After nearly 15 minutes of soul searching, I have heard the call. Nation, I will seek the office of the president of the United States. I am doing it!"[72]

Doing Too Well in the Polls

As the media picked up the story, Colbert's poll numbers started to actually climb, even beating some of his contenders: A Public Opinion Strategies national poll found that Colbert was drawing 2.3 percent of the support in the Democratic race, putting him ahead of serious candidates Bill Richardson and Dennis Kucinich, both at 2.1 percent, and putting him only slightly behind the future vice-president, Joe Biden, who was drawing 2.7 percent.

Colbert explains his decision to run for president during an appearance on NBC's Meet the Press *in 2007. Although his candidacy was ultimately not for real, it was an opportunity for Colbert to offer comment on the state of politics as entertainment.*

Momentum continued to build, and by the next week a Rasmussen poll showed that in a three-way race against Democrat Hillary Clinton and Republican Rudy Giuliani, the fake news pundit was drawing a remarkable 13 percent—far higher than most third-party candidates in previous presidential elections.

In fact, Colbert was doing so well in the polls that some did not appreciate the joke. Many argued that in using the presidential election to spread a comedic message, Colbert had crossed a line. A spokesman for Richardson, for example, said, "This is a serious election with serious consequences and we are not going to comment on this ridiculous exercise."[73] The Colbert Nation, on the other hand, was wildly supportive. Almost immediately, Colbert became an Internet sensation. A Facebook group called "1,000,000 Strong for Stephen T. Colbert" garnered over 850,000 members within a week of his announcement—the fastest-growing group in Facebook history to date.

Yet the run was not to be. After learning that it cost $35,000 to be included in the Republican primary in South Carolina, Colbert dropped plans to run as a Republican. He did pay $2,500 to run as a Democrat, but in the end, the South Carolina Democratic Party dropped him from the ballot. He acknowledged that the rejection stung, even though he joked until the very end: "They tell you when you're a child that anyone can run for President. But apparently not you, Stephen Colbert."[74]

Though Colbert was never serious about actually running for the presidency, the real support he garnered for his fake candidacy seemed to reflect the perception that politics has degenerated into a form of entertainment, of which many Americans have grown weary. Again and again, his comedy has a serious side that resonates with many mainstream Americans.

The March to Keep Fear Alive

In October 2010, Colbert further blurred the line between entertainment and politics, this time teaming up with Jon Stewart to satirize the way in which political speech in America has increasingly taken a hostile, paranoid, and exaggerated tone. The pair

Colbert appears on stage in a comedy bit from the "Rally to Restore Sanity and/or Fear," which he cohosted at the National Mall in Washington, D.C., with Jon Stewart in October 2010.

staged a protest in Washington, D.C., called the "Rally to Restore Sanity and/or Fear." It was intended to satirize other such events, such as the "Restoring Honor" rally held two months earlier by right-wing ideologue Glenn Beck, which had a strong religious focus and a conservative political agenda.

In contrast, the "Rally to Restore Sanity and/or Fear" was a plea for sanity and civility in political discourse. Part comedy festival, part concert, and part parody of media-hyped political rallies, Stewart and Colbert asked all those who "think shouting is annoying, counterproductive, and terrible for your throat; who feel that the loudest voices shouldn't be the only ones that get heard; and who believe that the only time it's appropriate to draw a Hitler mustache on someone is when that person is actually Hitler"[75] to join them in an effort to tone down the national dialogue on political and social issues. The event provided a perfect vehicle for the two comedians to lampoon American political divisions and the media's role in polarizing debates. It touched on many of the themes satirized by

Colbert's on-air persona—fear mongering, partisan punditry, and sensationalism.

Interestingly, Colbert's part of the rally was originally slated to be called the "Rally to Restore Truthiness." In an out-of-character interview shortly before the event, Colbert commented on the decision to keep the march primarily about fear:

I don't think we actually need to restore [truthiness]. I think it is perfectly healthy. I think if you just look around you, I doubt that many people in American politics are acting on facts. Everybody on both sides is acting on the things that move them emotionally the most. And that is the most successful way to behave. By keeping fear alive, we are keeping truthiness alive at the same time. Action out of emotion is all that truthiness is about—making your decisions based upon how you feel. Right now, it seems like fear is the strongest emotion that motivates us.[76]

The "Rally to Restore Sanity" was first announced on *The Daily Show* on September 16, 2010, when Stewart declared his intention to "take it down a notch for America."[77] The same night, on his show, Colbert declared his intention to have a "March to Keep Fear Alive" by saying, "I am sorry, Jon Stewart, I will not take it down a notch, I will take it up a skosh."[78] Colbert mockingly stated that he would participate in the rally only to uphold truthiness and fight Stewart's unnerving reasonableness.

The rally immediately gained support on the Internet, with over a quarter of a million people announcing they would attend. Those who would not make the trip to Washington, D.C., were offered satellite rallies in other major cities, including Chicago, San Francisco, Los Angeles, and Honolulu. Originally scheduled to take place in the area by the Washington Monument, expected turnout grew so large that the event was relocated to the east end of the National Mall, facing the Capitol. One estimate put the actual crowd at 215,000. In addition, the rally was broadcast live on Comedy Central and C-SPAN. The Comedy Central network alone drew an estimated 2 million viewers, as well as 570,000 who watched the live video stream of the event.

"I'm Pretty Sure You're Not Hitler"

The hundreds of thousands of people in attendance brought signs and costumes that expressed ironic political messages or pleas for more civil discourse. A group of people dressed as tea bags mocked the Tea Party, a conservative movement known for its

Many attendees of the "Rally to Restore Sanity and/or Fear" brought signs bearing silly, ironic, or poignant slogans that made fun of those seen at other "real" political events.

anti-immigration, antigovernment stance and support of what the Tea Party defines as traditional American values. Other rally attendees simply held signs to satirize American political views. Some featured slogans such as "Civil is sexy!" and "It's a sad day when our politicians are comical and I have to take our comedians seriously." One person's sign criticized the Christian religious message of many conservatives: "I wouldn't presume to tell God who he hates." Another sign ironically mocked the exaggerated, sometimes hysterical rhetoric (or hyperbole) found at other political rallies and in the media. It read, "People who use hyperbole should be shot!" Yet another sign, which parodied the trend of putting Hitler mustaches on images of political opponents, read, "I disagree with you, but I'm pretty sure you're not Hitler!"[79]

Musical celebrities joined the fun, including John Legend, Tony Bennett, Sheryl Crow, Kid Rock, R2-D2, Yusuf Islam (formerly known as Cat Stevens), and Ozzy Osbourne. Comedy sketches were woven throughout the program. In one example, Colbert gave out the Stephen Colbert Fear Award—a bronze medal made of a naked man running with scissors.

Since Colbert speaks only through his character, it was up to Stewart to make the serious closing remarks, which summarized the overriding theme of the rally: politicians are overly partisan, and the sensationalist media hypes and even creates issues for Americans to fear and fight about: "The country's 24-hour politico, pundit, perpetual panic conflictinator did not cause our problems. But its existence makes it that much harder. The press can hold its magnifying glass up to our own problems, bringing them into focus ... or they can use that magnifying glass to light ants on fire—and then perhaps host a week of shows on the sudden, unexpected, dangerous flaming-ant epidemic." Stewart was so moved by the turnout that he claimed, "Sanity will always be in the eye of the beholder. To see you here today and the kind of people that you are, has restored mine."[80]

Stewart and Colbert's joint venture gave voice to Americans fed up with current media and political tactics. As for Colbert, his persona had clearly become a national phenomenon that continued to gain support and become a force in and of itself.

Chapter 5

Colbert's Cultural Impact

Stephen Colbert's unique brand of satire has touched a nerve with a nation eager for someone to poke holes in the pretensions of politics and the media. As *The Colbert Report* continues to enjoy popularity, Colbert has had a unique cultural impact. He has used his fame to bring attention to important causes. He has highlighted social and political problems using humor and satire. By using the very forms of media he sometimes mocks on the show, he has been able to get his message out quickly and in a contemporary manner, and his fans have responded.

Entertaining Troops in the Persian Gulf

While Colbert pokes fun at the reasons the U.S. military is in Iraq and elsewhere, he remains a dedicated advocate of the soldiers in the effort. In June 2009, Colbert brought his show to Iraq and filmed a week's worth of episodes alongside U.S. troops stationed at Camp Victory in Baghdad. He humorously pointed out that many had been deployed to the beleaguered nation multiple times. "It must be nice here in Iraq because I understand some of you keep coming back again and again," he said. "You've earned so many frequent flyer miles, you've earned a free ticket to Afghanistan,"[81] where the United States has also been at war since 2001.

Colbert cringes as U.S. Army general Ray Odierno starts shaving his head during Colbert's appearance in Baghdad, Iraq, to perform for military personnel in 2009.

Wearing a suit and tie specially created for him in the army camouflage pattern, Colbert drew rousing applause when he showed a clip of himself going through a mock version of the army's basic training regimen. The highlight of the series occurred when one of Colbert's guests, General Ray Odierno, the commander of U.S. forces in Iraq, received a prerecorded message from the White House in which President Barack Obama jokingly "ordered" the commander to give Colbert a military haircut. The general acquiesced, and Colbert's head was shaved to thunderous applause.

A year later, in September 2010, Colbert offered another salute to the troops when he devoted two more episodes to honoring American service members in a special called "Been There, Won That: The Returnification of the American-Do Troopscape." As Colbert said, "No matter how you felt about this war, we Americans sent them off to fight it. And now that it's over, we should thank them. And quickly, because I think a lot of them are getting sent to Afghanistan."[82] The episodes were filmed in studio and featured high-profile guests, including Odierno and Vice President Joe Biden. The audience was filled with service members as well as active-duty members from Iraq and Afghanistan via satellite.

Congressional Testimony

Colbert continued to make his show a platform to keep important issues in the forefront. For example, he took on the issue of migrant labor and sought to raise awareness of the plight of migrant workers. Many such people work temporarily in the United States. They harvest crops during long hours, in the hot sun, and many live in unsanitary work camps. Colbert became intrigued by a campaign sponsored by the group United Farm Workers of America, which was fighting to give illegal immigrants a legal way to gain citizenship. The campaign, called "Take Our Jobs," gave Americans an opportunity to work the many agricultural jobs typically done by migrant workers. The point of the program was to show Americans how difficult, labor-intensive, and poorly paid agricultural jobs are, and that they do not in fact threaten American jobs, as is frequently charged.

Colbert spent a day on a farm in upstate New York crating corn and picking beans. Shortly after, in September 2010, Colbert testified before Congress on behalf of the United Farm Workers Union. He told the packed hearing room, "I like talking about people who don't have any power, and it seems like some of the

Colbert testifies in character before a congressional subcommittee on behalf of the United Farm Workers Union in 2010 to bring attention to the plight of migrant workers.

least powerful people in the United States are migrant workers who come and do our work but don't have any rights as a result." Describing his work in the fields as "really, really hard," Colbert went on to jokingly say, "This brief experience made me realize why so few Americans are clamoring to begin an exciting career as a migrant farm worker."[83]

While some commentators thought that Colbert had gone too far by testifying before Congress in character, others felt Colbert did exactly what he meant to do—bring attention to an important issue. As journalist Peter Grier put it:

> Never underestimate the power of pure attention. Hundreds of thousands (maybe millions) of Americans tomorrow will know more about the conditions in which migrants work because a comedian picked corn for a day. It doesn't matter that Colbert did not have a three-point plan for passing a bill that allows illegal migrant workers to work towards legal status by remaining in agricultural jobs. Today those workers are less faceless than they were before.[84]

By poking fun at the powers-that-be, Colbert harnesses enthusiasm for the issues he thinks are important. In the process, he leaves his wide audience better informed.

The Colbert Bump

Colbert continues to use the show to gain attention for everything from political causes, TV shows, and even products. From politicians to actors, guests on the show get so much media exposure that they often experience a surge in popularity.

Colbert coined this phenomenon "the Colbert bump" in 2006, after New York candidate John Hall appeared on the show in 2006 and went on to win a close election to the House of Representatives. Hall's Republican opponent, Sue Kelly, had declined invitations to appear on the show. Soon after, a political commentator speculated in the *American Prospect* that "her refusal to appear on cable's popular 'The Colbert Report' may

Colbert Super PAC

In 2011, Stephen Colbert once again inserted himself into the national political debate. Mocking the nation's campaign finance laws, Colbert announced he would pursue his own Super PAC, a type of political action committee organized to raise money to help elect political candidates or influence political issues. The comedian intends his Super PAC as a satire of the current campaign finance system, which allows for the creation of these political organizations that can receive unlimited corporate contributions that can be used to influence elections.

The parodist received rousing applause from his fans when he filed papers

Colbert speaks after attending a hearing before the Federal Election Commission to gain approval for the Colbert Super PAC in Washington, D.C.

at the Federal Election Commission on May 13, stating that "there should be unlimited campaign money, and I want some of it." Remaining in character, he followed with this statement: "I believe in the American Dream, and that dream is simple: That anyone, no matter who they are, if they are determined, if they are willing to work hard enough, someday they can grow up to create a legal entity which can then receive unlimited campaign funds which can be used to influence elections."

Source: Quoted in Dan Froomkin. "Stephen Colbert PAC: Fans Cheer Outside Federal Election Commission as Comedian Files Papers." Huffington Post, May 13, 2011. www.huffingtonpost.com/2011/05/13/stephen-colbert-pac-fans-cheer-outside-fec_n_861853.html.

have proved somewhat costly." To which Colbert responded, "Somewhat? All what. She could've gotten the 'Colbert bump,' instead she got the 'Colbert dump.'"[85] Fans have been touting Colbert's self-declared "bump" ever since.

Although difficult to quantify precisely, at least one study has confirmed that the Colbert bump—the upswing in popularity after appearing on the show—may be real. Political scientist James Fowler of the University of California, San Diego, studied the Colbert bump phenomenon. Fowler found that Democrats who appeared on the show got 44 percent more campaign dona-tions than those who do not appear on the show. Although this particular study suggests that the "bump" does not do as much for Republicans, former Arkansas governor Mike Huckabee credited his appearance on *The Colbert Report* with pushing him ahead in the 2008 Republican presidential primary race. Huckabee was happy to give Colbert credit for his surge in popularity, saying somewhat jokingly during a second appearance on the show: "The only reason I'm the front-runner now is because of the Colbert bump. If it were not for that I would be probably some-where serving hamburgers at a drive-in restaurant."[86]

Everything Colbert

Other indications of Colbert's influence and popularity are the many honors and accolades that have been bestowed upon him. In 2007, for example, Virgin American Airline, owned by the billionaire Richard Branson, christened one of its aircraft "Air Colbert" in honor of the comedian. Also in 2007, Ben & Jerry's ice cream honored him with a new flavor called Stephen Colbert's Americone Dream, vanilla ice cream with fudge covered waffle cone chunks and caramel. In reference to this honor, Colbert said, "I'm not afraid to say it. Dessert has a well-known liberal agenda. What I hope to do with this ice cream is bring some balance back to the freezer case."[87] All proceeds go to charity by the same name as the ice cream flavor. Other such examples include:

- In 2006 breeders at the San Francisco zoo named a baby bald eagle Stephen Jr. Throughout the year, Colbert periodically reported on the health of the bird, which was reintroduced into the wild in 2006.

- In 2008, East Carolina University biologist Jason Bond named a new species of trapdoor spider *Aptostichus stephencolberti* in tribute to Colbert.
- In 2009, NASA held an online poll to name a node on the space station. Online voters had chosen the name "Colbert," but NASA chose "Tranquility" instead. In an April 2009 episode of the *Report*, NASA astronaut Surita Williams announced that NASA would instead install a Combined Operational Load-Bearing External Resistance Treadmill (COLBERT) on the Space Station.
- In 2009, researchers at the University of California, Santa Cruz, named a pair of elephant seals *Stelephant Colbert* and *Jon Sealwart*.
- In 2009, the mayor of San Jose named a falcon roosting on City Hall *Esteban Colbert*; the falcon is monitored on the city's FalconCam, which was installed on the roof of City Hall a few years before.

Colbert, second from right, poses with ice cream moguls Ben Cohen, left, and Jerry Greenfield to introduce a new flavor called Stephen Colbert's Americone Dream in 2007.

Colbert's Other Work

Although best known as the host of *The Colbert Report,* Stephen Colbert has lent his talents to many other projects: In 2003, he coauthored the satirical novel *Wigfield: The Can-Do Town That Just May Not* and performed in a stage adaptation the same year. Other acting credits

Colbert, left, appeared in the 2005 movie Bewitched with Jim Turner, Will Ferrell, and Jason Schwartzman.

include a small supporting role in the 2005 film adaptation of *Bewitched* and a role in the film adaptation of *Strangers with Candy* the same year. In November 2008, his Christmas special *A Colbert Christmas: The Greatest Gift of All* aired on Comedy Central. Over the years, he has made guest appearances on several television series, including *Spin City, Law & Order: Criminal Intent, The Simpsons,* and on the improvisational comedy show *Whose Line Is It Anyway?* In 2011 Colbert had a costarring role in Stephen Sondheim's *Company* revival on Broadway.

Colbert has also provided the vocals for various animated projects, including *Harvey Birdman, Attorney at Law; The Venture Bros; Crank Yankers; Saturday Night Live's* "TV Funhouse"; and the animated movie *Monsters vs. Aliens.*

A Colbert Lexicon

One of the most concrete ways Colbert has become a part of America's cultural landscape is that many of the words he has coined on the show get picked up in the media and end up entering the popular lexicon. While the most enduring may be "truthiness," there are a host of others.

Colbert uses his wit to develop a word or catchphrase that mocks a larger trend he sees in American society. For example, Colbert developed the term "Wikiality" to mock America's tendency to rely on the editable online encyclopedia Wikipedia, where, as he puts it, "any user can change any entry, and if enough users agree with them, it becomes true."[88] He introduced the term, a blend of "reality" and "Wiki," during his July 31, 2006, Wørd segment, saying that "together we can create a reality that we all agree on—the reality we just agreed on."[89] Through Wikiality,

Coining Words

Since introducing "truthiness" on the show's debut episode, Colbert has continued to come up with more new words, often by blending two or more unrelated ones. The following Colbert gems are among those recorded in the Urban Dictionary, an online repository of streetwise words and phrases posted and defined by readers:

Freem: To take the "do" out of "freedom."

Lincolnish: Like Abraham Lincoln.

Superstantial: Being the essence of a lack of substance.

Eneagled: Endowed with eagle-like qualities.

Psychopharmaparenting: The increasing tendency of parents to medicate their children with pharmaceutical drugs for every little perceived behavioral abnormality their children exhibit even though such behaviors (such as restlessness) are normal.

Southsourcing: Instead of hiring illegal aliens to work for you in this country, this is the business practice of relocating your manufacturing and labor pool to Mexico—so everything is just as cheap, and nice and legal.

Source: The Urban Dictionary. www.urbandictionary.com.

Colbert brilliantly skewers the idea that the truth is whatever Wikipedia users say it is. "Wikiality is the idea that something *becomes* true if enough people say it," explains Ethan Mills in the book *Stephen Colbert and Philosophy*. "'Stephen doesn't like being told that George Washington owned slaves, but through wikiality it can become true that Washington was not a slave owner!"[90]

Continuing the wiki theme, Colbert has also coined "Wikilobbying," when "money determines Wikipedia entries, reality has become a commodity."[91] Colbert is referring to a case in which Microsoft allegedly paid someone to alter a Wikipedia entry to cast the company in a more favorable light.

Colbert has also coined the term "wordinista," which he defines disparagingly as anyone who sticks up for the proper use of the English language. Defending truthiness, Colbert declared, "What is it with you wordinistas telling me what is and isn't a word?"[92] As Jason Southworth, a philosophy instructor at Fort Hays State University in Kansas, describes it:

> From the context, it is clear that one thing a wordinista does is tell people what is and is not a word. This isn't enough to capture the whole meaning of the term, however. The "What is it with you" prior to the term also implies that the word is meant to have a negative connotation. … The "inista" part of the word should make most people immediately think of the word "Sandinista" … a radical Marxist political party from Nicaragua. So, it seems "wordinista" is also intended to suggest a radical disposition. Putting these things together, a "wordinista" is a person who is radical about correcting others about their misuse of words and their use of non-established words.[93]

Colbert's lexiconography is popular but also telling. As Adam Sternbergh of *New York* magazine has said:

> Colbertisms ring throughout the land—and not just from the mouth of Colbert. The best testament to the triumph of the Colbertocracy is that you can now hear a Colbert line like "I believe the government that governs best is the

government that governs least, and by these standards, we have set up a fabulous government in Iraq" and devoid of context, you might genuinely wonder if it came from a parodist, a pundit, or from the president himself.[94]

A Lasting Impact

As many reviewers of *The Colbert Report* have pointed out, American media analysts and politicians all seem to be in character; Colbert just makes his a bit more obvious. As satire, Colbert comes so close to mocking the real deal that he is like the traditional fool to the king—getting the monarch to see his flaws by making fun of him in an exaggerated way. Colbert has a way of showing the emperor has no clothes, and Americans seem to embrace the concept fully. As Colbert has said in urging Americans not to accept the status quo, "This is not a dream, you are not going to wake up from this."[95]

Introduction: A New Twist on an Old Concept

1. Quoted in Ken Plume. "An Interview with Stephen Colbert." IGN.com, August 11, 2003. http://movies.ign.com/articles/ 433/433111p1.html.
2. Aaron Allen Schiller, ed. *Stephen Colbert and Philosophy: I Am Philosophy (And So Can You!).* Chicago: Open Court, 2009, p. xii.

Chapter 1: The Tragic Road to Comedy

3. Quoted in MUSC Library. "With Integrity and Dignity: The Life of James W. Colbert, Jr., MD." 2011. www.waring.library .musc.edu/exhibits/colbert.
4. Quoted in David Cote. "As He Prepares to Move On from *The Daily Show*, the Host of the Upcoming *Colbert Report* Gets His Ulysses On." *Time Out New York*, June 9–15, 2005. newyork .timeout.com/arts-culture/651563/joyce-words.
5. Quoted in Neil Strauss. "Stephen Colbert on Deconstructing the News, Religion, and the Colbert Nation." *Rolling Stone*, September 2, 2009. www.rollingstone.com/culture/news/ stephen-colbert-on-deconstructing-the-news-religion-and- the-colbert-nation-20090902.
6. Quoted in Deborah Solomon. "Funny About the News." *New York Times*, September 25, 2005. www.nytimes.com/2005/09/25/ magazine/25questions.html?pagewanted=print.
7. Quoted in Robin Finn. "Public Lives: Covering the Convention for Laughs." *New York Times,* August 27, 2004. www.nytimes. com/2004/08/27/nyregion/public-lives-covering-the-convention -for- laughs.html.
8. Quoted in Bryce Donovan. "Great Charlestonian? … Or the Greatest Charlestonian? Stephen Colbert." *Post and Courier*, April 29, 2006. www.postandcourier.com/stories/ ?newsID=83674.

9. Quoted in Daniel Schorn. "The Colbert Report." CBS News, April 27, 2006. www.cbsnews.com/stories/2006/04/27/60minutes/main1553506.shtml?tag=contentMain;content Body.
10. Quoted in Donovan. "Great Charlestonian? … Or the Greatest Charlestonian? Stephen Colbert."
11. Quoted in *Parade*. "If You Are Laughing, You Can't Be Afraid." September 23, 2007. www.parade.com/articles/editions/2007/edition_09-23-2007/AStephen_Colbert.
12. Quoted in Plume. "An Interview with Stephen Colbert."
13. Quoted in Nathan Rabin. "Interview: Stephen Colbert." AV Club, January 25, 2006. www.avclub.com/articles/stephen-colbert,13970/.
14. Quoted in Plume. "An Interview with Stephen Colbert."
15. Quoted in Rabin. "Interview: Stephen Colbert."
16. Quoted in Rabin. "Interview: Stephen Colbert."
17. Quoted in Cate Plys. "The Real Stephen Colbert." *Northwestern*, Winter 2010. www.northwestern.edu/magazine/winter2010/feature/the-real-stephen-colbert.html.
18. Quoted in Plys. "The Real Stephen Colbert."
19. Quoted in Plys. "The Real Stephen Colbert."
20. Quoted in Plys. "The Real Stephen Colbert."
21. Quoted in Plume. "An Interview with Stephen Colbert."
22. Quoted in Plys. "The Real Stephen Colbert."

Chapter 2: *The Daily Show* Years

23. Quoted in Plume. "An Interview with Stephen Colbert."
24. Quoted in Elana Berkowitz and Amy Schiller."Five Minutes with Stephen Colbert." Campus Progress, July 11, 2005. http://campusprogress.org/articles/stephen_colbert/.
25. Quoted in Plume. "An Interview with Stephen Colbert."
26. Quoted in Plume. "An Interview with Stephen Colbert."
27. Quoted in Jacqueline Schneider. "So What Do You Do, Stephen Colbert?" Media Bistro, May 6, 2003. www.mediabistro.com/articles/cache/a238.asp.
28. *The Daily Show with Jon Stewart*. Comedy Central, August 15, 2002.

29. Quoted in Berkowitz and Schiller. "Five Minutes with Stephen Colbert."
30. Quoted in *Parade*. "If You Are Laughing, You Can't Be Afraid."
31. Quoted in Schneider. "So What Do You Do, Stephen Colbert?"
32. Quoted in Finn. "Public Lives: Covering the Convention for Laughs."
33. Quoted in Schneider. "So What Do You Do, Stephen Colbert?"
34. Quoted in Finn. "Public Lives: Covering the Convention for Laughs."
35. Quoted in Jake Coyle. "The 'Colbert Report' Behind the Scenes." Huffington Post, June 9, 2008. www.huffingtonpost .com/2008/06/09/the-colbert-report-behind_n_105988.html.
36. Quoted in Marc Peyser. "The Truthiness Teller." *Newsweek*, February 12, 2006. www.newsweek.com/2006/02/12/ the-truthiness-teller.html.

Chapter 3: *The Colbert Report*

37. Quoted in Johnny Frohlichstein. "Pundit Face-Off: Stewart vs. Colbert." The Kirkwood Call, April 20, 2011. www. thekirkwoodcall.com/opinion/2011/04/20/pundit-face-off-stewart-vs-colbert/.
38. Quoted in Plys. "The Real Stephen Colbert."
39. Nancy Franklin. "The Spinoff Zone." *New Yorker,* November 28, 2005. www.newyorker.com/archive/2005/11/28/051128crte_ television.
40. Quoted in Peyser. "The Truthiness Teller."
41. Quoted in Jake Coyle. "Colbert's 'Report' Rapport Still Strong." *Seattle Times*, July 7, 2008. http://seattletimes.nwsource.com/ html/television/2008035067_colbertreport07.html.
42. *The Colbert Report*. Comedy Central, October 17, 2005.
43. Mark Peters. "Mark Peters on the Colbert Suffix." *Good Magazine,* no. 007, October 3, 2007. www.good.is/post/ mark-peters-on-the-colbert-suffix/.
44. *The Colbert Report*. Comedy Central, October 17, 2005.
45. Quoted in Adam Sternbergh. "Stephen Colbert Has America by the Ballots." *New York Magazine*, October 8, 2006. http:// nymag.com/news/politics/22322/.

46. Quoted in Adam Gorlick. "Colbert's 'Truthiness' Pronounced Word of the Year." *Houston Chronicle*, December 8, 2006. www.chron.com/disp/story.mpl/chronicle/4389349.html.

47. Quoted in Schiller, ed. *Stephen Colbert and Philosophy*, p. 111.

48. Ben Zimmer. "Truthiness." *New York Times*, October 13, 2010. www.nytimes.com/2010/10/17/magazine/17FOB-onlanguage-t.html.

49. Quoted in Sternbergh. "Stephen Colbert Has America by the Ballots."

50. Quoted in Sternbergh. "Stephen Colbert Has America by the Ballots."

51. *The Colbert Report*. Comedy Central, October 17, 2005.

52. Quoted in Plys. "The Real Stephen Colbert."

53. *The Colbert Report*. Comedy Central, July 31, 2006.

54. *The Colbert Report*. Comedy Central, February 28, 2011.

55. Quoted in Matea Gold. "The Truly Serious Appear on 'The Colbert Report.'" *Los Angeles Times*, March 27, 2006. http://articles.latimes.com/2006/mar/27/entertainment/et-humor27.

56. *The Colbert Report*. Comedy Central, November 15, 2003.

57. Steven Daly. "Stephen Colbert: The Second Most Powerful Idiot in America." *Telegraph*, May 18, 2008. www.telegraph.co.uk/culture/tvandradio/3673509/Stephen-Colbert-the-second-most-powerful-idiot-in-America.html.

58. Quoted in Daly. "Stephen Colbert: The Second Most Powerful Idiot in America."

59. Quoted in Plys. "The Real Stephen Colbert."

60. Quoted in Seth Mnookin. "The Man in the Iron Mask." *Vanity Fair*, October 2007. www.vanityfair.com/culture/features/2007/10/colbert200710.

Chapter 4: Colbert Unleashed

61. Quoted in Jacques Steinberg. "After Press Dinner, the Blogosphere Is Alive with the Sound of Colbert Chatter." *New York Times*, May 3, 2006. www.nytimes.com/2006/05/03/arts/03colb.html.

62. Quoted in Sternbergh. "Stephen Colbert Has America by the Ballots."
63. Quoted in Sternbergh. "Stephen Colbert Has America by the Ballots."
64. Quoted in Sternbergh. "Stephen Colbert Has America by the Ballots."
65. Frank Rich. "Throw the Truthiness Bums Out." *New York Times,* November 5, 2006. http://select.nytimes.com/2006/11/05/opinion/05rich.html.
66. Quoted in Sternbergh. "Stephen Colbert Has America by the Ballots."
67. Quoted in James Poniewozik. "Stephen Colbert and the Death of 'The Room.'" Tuned In, *Time,* May 3, 2006. http://tunedin.blogs.time.com/2006/05/03/stephen_colbert_and_the_death/.
68. Quoted in Strauss. "Stephen Colbert on Deconstructing the News, Religion, and the Colbert Nation."
69. Matt Frisch. "Colbert Boosts U.S. Speed Skating Team." CNN Entertainment, November 3, 2009. http://articles.cnn.com/2009-11-03/entertainment/stephen.colbert.winter.olympics_1_colbert-nation-colbert-report-host-stephen-colbert?_s=PM:SHOWBIZ.
70. Sternbergh. "Stephen Colbert Has America by the Ballots."
71. Maureen Dowd and Stephen Colbert. "A Mock Columnist, Amok." *New York Times*, October 14, 2007. www.nytimes.com/2007/10/14/opinion/14dowd.html.
72. *The Colbert Report.* Comedy Central, October 16, 2007.
73. Quoted in Tom Baldwin. "Making the Campaign into a Running Joke." *Times* (London), October 27, 2007. www.timesonline.co.uk/tol/news/world/us_and_americas/article2748888.ece.
74. Quoted in Rachel Sklar. "Colbert—and His Wife—Rock the *New Yorker Fest.* " Huffington Post, October 6, 2008. www.huffingtonpost.com/2008/10/06/stephen-colbert-at-the-em_n_132019.html.
75. Rally to Restore Sanity, September 9, 2010. www.rallytorestoresanity.com.

76. Quoted in Ben Zimmer. "Truthiness." *New York Times*, October 13, 2010. www.nytimes.com/2010/10/17/magazine/17FOB-onlanguage-t.html.

77. *The Daily Show with Jon Stewart*. Comedy Central, September 16, 2010.

78. *The Colbert Report*. Comedy Central, September 16, 2010.

79. Quoted in Katla McGlynn. "The Funniest Signs from the Rally to Restore Sanity and/or Fear." Huffington Post, October 30, 2010. www.huffingtonpost.com/2010/10/30/the-funniest-signs-at-the_n_776490.html#s169371&title=Nope.

80. Jon Stewart. "Keynote Address at the Rally to Restore Sanity." American Rhetoric, October 30, 2010. www.americanrhetoric.com/speeches/jonstewartsanityrallykeynote.htm.

Chapter 5: Colbert's Cultural Impact

81. Quoted in Kim Gamel. "In Iraq, Colbert Shaves His Head, Declares Victory." *Army Times*, June 8, 2009. www.armytimes.com/news/2009/06/ap_colbert_iraq_060809/.

82. Quoted in Dave Itzkoff. "Colbert to Welcome Home Iraq Troops with Specials." *New York Times*, August 21, 2010. www.nytimes.com/2010/08/21/arts/television/21arts-COLBERTTOWEL_BRF.html.

83. Peter Grier. "Stephen Colbert on Capitol Hill: Did He Help Migrant Workers?" *Christian Science Monitor*, September 24, 2010. www.csmonitor.com/USA/Elections/Vox-News/2010/0924/Stephen-Colbert-on-Capitol-Hill-Did-he-help-migrant-workers.

84. Grier. "Stephen Colbert on Capitol Hill."

85. Quoted in Andrea Thompson. "Science Confirms 'the Colbert Bump.'" *Today*, MSNBC, April 18, 2008. http://today.msnbc.msn.com/id/24202466/ns/today-today_tech/t/science-confirms-colbert-bump/.

86. Quoted in Huffington Post. "Huckabee Seeks Another 'Colbert Bump.'" January 10, 2008. www.huffingtonpost.com/2008/01/10/huckabee-seeks-another-co_n_80892.html.

87. Quoted in Associated Press, "New Ice Cream Named for Stephen Colbert," *The Washington Post*, February 14, 2007. www.washingtonpost.com/wp-dyn/content/article/2007/02/14/AR2007021400985.html

88. *The Colbert Report*. Comedy Central, July 31, 2006.
89. *The Colbert Report*. Comedy Central, July 31, 2006.
90. Quoted in Schiller, ed. *Stephen Colbert and Philosophy*, p. 105.
91. *The Colbert Report*. Comedy Central, January 29, 2007.
92. *The Colbert Report*. Comedy Central, October 17, 2005.
93. Quoted in Schiller, ed. *Stephen Colbert and Philosophy*, p. 69.
94. Sternbergh. "Stephen Colbert Has America by the Ballots."
95. Quoted in Carr. "The Media Equation: The Gospel According to Mr. Colbert."

Important Dates

1964

Stephen Colbert is born on May 13, 1964.

1974

Colbert's father and two brothers are killed in an airplane crash.

1982

Enrolls in the all-male Hampden-Sydney College in Virginia.

1984

Transfers to Northwestern University's School of Speech as a theater major; begins performing improvisation with the No Fun Mud Piranhas, the campus improv team, and at the Annoyance Theater in Chicago.

1986

Graduates from Northwestern University; performs with Second City comedy troupe in Chicago.

1995

Develops *Exit 57*, a comedy sketch show that runs on Comedy Central.

1996

Works briefly as a cast member and writer on *The Dana Carvey Show* and as a freelance writer for *Saturday Night Live*.

1997

Joins the cast of *The Daily Show* as a correspondent character.

1998

Develops and performs in *Strangers with Candy*, a comedy series picked up by Comedy Central.

2000

Covers the presidential election season as part of *The Daily Show*'s award-winning coverage; performs voice-over work for the Cartoon Network animated series *Harvey Birdman, Attorney at Law*.

2003

Coauthors the satirical novel *Wigfield: The Can-Do Town That Just May Not*.

2004

Along with the cast of *The Daily Show*, covers the presidential election; shares the Emmy Award for Outstanding Writing on *The Daily Show*.

2005

Hosts *The Colbert Report* on Comedy Central; appears in a film adaptation of *Strangers with Candy*; also appears in a supporting role in the movie *Bewitched*; receives a second Emmy Award for writing on *The Daily Show*.

2006

Colbert gives a much publicized keynote speech at the White House Correspondents' Association dinner; wins a third Emmy Award for writing on *The Daily Show*; Merriam-Webster names "truthiness" its 2006 Word of the Year; *Time* names Colbert to its TIME 100 list of the world's most influential people; receives an honorary doctorate in fine arts from Knox College in Illinois.

2007

Ben & Jerry's releases a new ice cream flavor, Stephen Colbert's Americone Dream; Colbert announces his presidential candidacy in October; in November, the South Carolina Democratic Party votes to keep Colbert's name off the ballot; publishes his best-selling satirical book *I Am America (And So Can You!)*; the Associated Press names Colbert Celebrity of the Year.

2008

Receives a Peabody Award for *The Colbert Report*; receives an Emmy Award for writing for *The Colbert Report*; Colbert's Christmas special, *A Colbert Christmas: The Greatest Gift of All!*, airs on Comedy Central and is later released to DVD.

2009

Under the guise "Operation Iraqi Stephen: Going Commando," Colbert tapes a week's worth of shows at Camp Victory in Baghdad; the commander of U.S. forces in Iraq shaves Colbert's head military style as part of the routine; signs a sponsorship agreement with the U.S. Olympic speed skating team after the team loses a prominent sponsor.

2010

Participates in the United Farm Workers' "Take Our Jobs" program, during which he spends a day picking vegetables with migrant farm workers; later testifies on behalf of migrant workers before the House Judiciary Subcommittee on Immigration, Citizenship, and Border Security; receives a Grammy Award for Best Comedy Album for *A Colbert Christmas: The Greatest Gift of All!*; along with Jon Stewart, hosts the Rally to Restore Sanity and/or Fear in Washington, D.C.

2011

Files papers to launch his own political action committee to draw attention to campaign finance laws; joins a Charleston-to-Bermuda yachting race as captain of the sailboat *Spirit of Juno*, finishing second.

Books

Stephen Colbert. *I Am America (And So Can You!)*. New York: Grand Central Publishing, 2007. A collection of Colbert's comedic musings on the things that are wrong with America.

Stephen Colbert et al. *Stephen Colbert's Tek Jansen*. Portland, OR: Oni, 2007. A compilation of the comic book series that follows the adventures of science fiction hero Tek Jansen as he battles the enemies of freedom.

Stephen Colbert et al. *Wigfield: The Can-Do Town That Just May Not*. New York: Hyperion, 2003. This book tells the story of the small town of Wigfield and the cast of comedic characters who inhabit it.

Aaron Allen Schiller, ed. *Stephen Colbert and Philosophy: I Am Philosophy (And So Can You!)*. Chicago: Open Court, 2009. A collection of essays that expounds on the comedy of Stephen Colbert.

Periodicals

Stephen Colbert. "Stephen Colbert's (Shocking!) Secrets of the (Very!) Extreme." *Outside Magazine*, May 6, 2011.

Ana Marie Cox. "Was Stephen Colbert Funny?" *Time*, May 4, 2006.

Maureen Dowd. "America's Anchors." *Rolling Stone*, November 16, 2006.

Dan Froomkin. "The Colbert Blackout." *Washington Post*, May 2, 2006.

Joshua Green. "The Colbert Notion." *Atlantic*, October 19, 2007.

Howard Kurtz. "TV's Newest Anchor: A Smirk in Progress." *Washington Post*, October 10, 2005.

Troy Patterson. "Why Stephen Colbert Didn't Bomb in DC." *Slate*, May 2, 2006.

Alexandra Petri. "Peace Trains, Crazy Trains, Love Trains and Automobiles at Stewart Rally." *Washington Post*, October 30, 2010.

Marc Peyer. "The Truthiness Teller." *Newsweek,* February 13, 2006.

David Remnick. "Reporter Guy." *New Yorker*, July 25, 2005.

Jacques Steinberg. "Candidate Colbert." *New York Times*, October 17, 2007.

Adam Sternbergh. "Stephen Colbert Has America by the Ballots." *New York Magazine*, October 8, 2006.

Ben Zimmer. "Truthiness." *New York Times*, October 13, 2010.

Internet Sources

Neal Conan. "Comedy as News." NPR, March 1, 2004. www.npr .org/templates/story/story.php?storyId=1739768&ps=rs.

Alex Knott. "Stephen Colbert Files FEC Request for Colbert PAC." Roll Call, May 12, 2011. http://www.rollcall.com/news/ Stephen-Colbert-PAC-FEC-video-205563-1.html.

Charlotte Laws. "What We Learned from Stephen Colbert's Presidential Campaign." CounterPunch, November 7, 2007. www.counterpunch.org/laws11072007.html.

Seth Mnookin. "The Man in the Iron Mask." *Vanity Fair*, October 2007. www.vanityfair.com/contributors/seth-mnookin.

Cate Plys. "The Real Stephen Colbert." *Northwestern Magazine,* Winter 2010. www.northwestern.edu/magazine/winter2010/ feature/the-real-stephen-colbert.html.

Robert Siegel. "'Daily Show' Correspondent Readies 'The Colbert Report.'" NPR, May 4, 2005. www.npr.org/templates/story/ story.php?storyId=4630860&ps=rs

Lam Thuy Vo. "Stephen Colbert for President." *Wall Street Journal*, November 4, 2008. http://online.wsj.com/article/ SB122564868967191179.html.

Kenneth P. Vogel. "Stephen Colbert at the FEC? Really." Politico, May 13, 2011. www.politico.com/news/stories/0511/54946.html

Josh Wolk. "Jon Stewart and Stephen Colbert: Mock the Vote." *Entertainment Weekly*, September 30, 2008. www.ew.com/ew/ article/0,,20228603,00.html.

Videos and DVDs

A Colbert Christmas: The Greatest Gift of All. Comedy Central, November 23, 2008. Colbert's Christmas special parodies Christmas variety shows, featuring many celebrity guests, including Elvis Costello, Willie Nelson, Jon Stewart, and others. The DVD was released two days after its Comedy Central debut.

Strangers with Candy. Comedy Central, April 7, 1999. This series, which ran from April 1999 to October 2000, spoofs the after-school specials of the 1970s and 1980s. It tells the story of forty-six-year-old Jerri Blank, who became a "boozer, a user, and a loser" after dropping out of high school as a teenager. Colbert plays history teacher Chuck Noblet. The complete series was released to DVD in 2006.

Websites

The Daily Show with Jon Stewart (www.thedailyshow.com). The official home of *The Daily Show* online. The site includes a searchable archive of video clips that feature Stephen Colbert as a correspondent and as a character in other skits.

The Colbert Nation (www.thecolbertnation.com). The official home of *The Colbert Report* online. The site includes a searchable archive of video clips from Colbert's debut show to the present, as well as highlights and full episodes of recent shows.

About the Author

Bonnie Szumski has been an editor and author of nonfiction books for over 25 years. Jill Karson has been a writer and editor of nonfiction books for young adults for 15 years.